AF580610

LIVING,
TOGETHER

LIVING, TOGETHER

REIMAGINING COMMUNITY IN THE AGE OF DISCONNECTION

EDITED BY

SAMANTHA PAIGE ROSEN

BEACON PRESS, BOSTON

BEACON PRESS
24 Farnsworth Street
Boston, Massachusetts
www.beacon.org

Beacon Press books
are published under the auspices of
the Unitarian Universalist Association of Congregations.

Printed in the United States of America

29 28 27 26 8 7 6 5 4 3 2 1

This book is printed on acid-free paper that meets the uncoated paper
ANSI/NISO specifications for permanence as revised in 1992.

Text design and composition by Kim Arney

Library of Congress Cataloguing-in-Publication
Data is available for this title.
Hardcover ISBN: 978-0-8070-2129-3
E-book ISBN: 978-0-8070-2130-9
Audiobook: 978-0-8070-2459-1

The authorized representative in the EU for product safety and
compliance is Easy Access System Europe 16879218, Mustamäe tee 50,
10621 Tallinn, Estonia: https://beacon.org/eu-contact.

For anyone with the
courage to imagine more.

And for Maisy and Deacon.

I have always felt that a human being
could only be saved by another human being.
I am aware that we do not save each other very often.
But I am also aware that we save each other some of the time.

—JAMES BALDWIN

CONTENTS

INTRODUCTION

HOME IS OTHER PEOPLE

The key to a good life isn't necessarily two adults and a couple of kids separated from the rest of the world by four walls. Not only is this version of the American Dream less accessible than ever, it's not what many of us need.

I'm writing this from my childhood bedroom, where I lived from ages seven to eighteen, and then again from twenty-nine to almost thirty-five. When I tell people my housemates are my parents, I typically get one of two reactions. Some pause, raise their eyebrows, smile wide, and ask if I think I'll move out soon. I'm used to it; I've prepared a response that I've practiced delivering confidently, sans apology. It begins, "It's actually been great for all of us . . ." and ends with ". . . I'm still plenty independent and social." Others get it, and might share that they stayed with grandparents for a few years in their twenties, or that a sibling recently moved back in with their parents.

Those of us who have experienced communal living or witnessed it firsthand know the benefits it can bring. The messaging in American culture that living independently, whether alone or with a nuclear family of your own creation, is an important milestone, even an achievement, is nearly inescapable. But many of us are learning that approach doesn't work—not for everyone and not for all the seasons of our adult lives.

Growing up in an upper-middle-class, majority-white suburb of Philadelphia, I was subject to the usual messages. I imagined that in my twenties, I'd live with roommates or alone before marrying a man and buying a single-family house together like the ones in my neighborhood. While I had friends and was part of artistic communities, these things weren't yet central to my vision for the future. I mostly daydreamed about partnership, education, and career achievements, as every sitcom I watched, magazine I read, and teacher I had told me to. I drank the American Dream Kool-Aid. And a lot of it.

I spent the first decade of my adult life chasing that dream, stamping out feelings of loneliness in service of my ambitions as I moved across the country and back again. Without established friends nearby, I sought out roommates on Craigslist and in Facebook groups, and while we occasionally shared meals, car rides, or dating horror stories, these actions were mostly logistical. We didn't become friends. It always seemed strange to live with someone I wasn't close to emotionally, so when it became financially possible to get my own apartment, I did.

At twenty-eight, the burnout hit. I watched many of my peers settle down with partners and start their own nuclear families; meanwhile, I was living alone—well, with my cats—and unexpectedly working through my sexuality. I was also at the end of a string of toxic jobs that eroded my mental health and exacerbated my chronic neck and back pain. After months of trying to continue working full-time, improve my well-being and explore my identity, and search for a new job, all while facing a 10 percent rent increase, it became clear I couldn't do it anymore.

What I didn't know then was that I wasn't alone in these difficulties. Today, younger generations in particular find themselves unable to afford homes, and even rent, and loneliness has become an epidemic. And while these are relatively modern-day developments—in the late 1990s, Carrie Bradshaw, of the television show *Sex and the City*, earned around $60,000–$70,000 a year as a newspaper columnist, and her New York City studio apartment would have cost around $1,000 in monthly rent; now she'd be paid roughly the same, but her rent would cost $3,000–$4,000—these issues have long been present for specific groups of people.[1] Living in a single-family household, whether with a nuclear family or alone, has consistently worked best for the white and wealthy, who can hire cleaners, tutors, babysitters, therapists, and coaches to supplement labor and care. It's ideal, too, for those who are younger and able-bodied, and often don't need the built-in physical and emotional support that chronically ill or older folks do—which I was beginning to see for myself. As my depression and anxiety, ADHD, and back problems worsened, I struggled to manage day-to-day responsibilities, like focusing at my full-time content writing job and standing without pain for long enough to cook anything that didn't come from the Trader Joe's frozen food aisle.

In the summer of 2019, I quit my job to focus on my health and moved back in with my parents. I was hesitant, but they encouraged it. I was so ashamed to be asking for help; I felt like I was giving up on all the things I had spent my adolescence and young adulthood working for. But for the first time in a long time, I also felt hope. I was looking for relief of all kinds—emotional, mental, physical, financial—and I sensed that living alongside people I cared about, and who cared about me, was going to make a difference in my quality of life.

My mom, my dad, and I actively worked to make each other's days easier and better. Instead of doing all the household chores myself, I focused on what I was best at and enjoyed most, and they did the same. At dinnertime, my mom cooked, my dad did the dishes, and I took out the trash. I embraced the ease of eating dinner together in front of the TV and the ridiculousness of spontaneously breaking out into song while cleaning up—things I could do alone, sure, but they just weren't as fun without company.

While many people, including my own sisters, might shudder at the idea of being around their mom and dad all the time, the arrangement didn't make me feel like a kid again, running through the same parental role-playing we'd engaged in throughout my childhood.

Rather, the move strengthened a different side of our relationship: these two people were my friends. Slightly overbearing friends, perhaps too concerned about whether or not I took a sweater when I went out, but friends nonetheless. The polite and distant roommate relationships of my twenties faded away as I leaned into the raucous laughter over inside jokes, the communal care, and yes, the almost dizzying comfort of having someone else to go food shopping, decide what's for dinner, and then make it. Imagine! All of this was doubly meaningful during those early months of the pandemic; my parents became the only people I could be closer than six feet from.

As I repaired my health and began making a steady income again as a freelance writer and writing tutor rather than an employee climbing the career ladder, I felt pressure to get my own place. I internalized people's expectations that I should move out. That I should live alone. After gatherings at friends' houses, I'd frantically scroll through apartments on Zillow, searching for my dream space. Still, I never took the plunge. I continued to stay with my parents, much longer than I imagined I would. A few years went by before I understood that I wasn't moving out because I simply didn't want to. I deleted the Zillow app from my phone.

But change is inevitable. In 2024, my parents decided they wanted to retire and downsize the following year. Living together was so transformative that we chose to buy two separate townhouses in the same complex—something I was able to do because I'd saved money on rent and utilities while at their house—so we could maintain some of the routines and systems of care we'd grown accustomed to. At this moment, I'm weeks away from moving there. And while my parents will follow in a few months, I'd be lying if I said I wasn't a little sad to be living alone again. The arrangement we've had for the past six years filled a hole that I was taught could exclusively be filled by a traditional nuclear family consisting of me, a partner, and children. Now I know that's not true.

My story is just one example of the many different ways communal living can enhance the material conditions of our lives and foster improved health, stronger relationships, and a genuine sense of connection. When *Catapult* magazine published an essay I wrote in 2022 about moving back in with my parents, I heard from readers in all sorts of living situations who connected with the idea that the key to a good life isn't necessarily two adults and a couple of kids separated from the rest of the world by four walls. Not only is this version of the American Dream less accessible than ever, but it's also not what many of us need—and it hasn't been for decades.

In 1970, 67 percent of Americans ages twenty-five to forty-nine were living in a nuclear family. Today, that number is closer to 37 percent.[2] The data doesn't lie. The nuclear family has been in decline for the last nearly sixty years, in large part because our country's circumstances have changed dramatically since the prosperity of the post-WWII period. But where are the stories of the growing number of people turning to other ways of organizing their lives and care networks? Living communally has become a more prominent topic in the media since the pandemic and the surge in housing prices over the past few years. Still, despite the fact that communal living is more relevant than it has ever been, we're often not hearing directly from those who have experienced it, who can capture in their own words the comforts and inconveniences, the trade-offs and delights. This anthology aims to fill that gap.

My goal in embarking on *Living, Together* was to gather a breadth of narratives that offer a window into how people in the US are incorporating support and connection into their everyday lives through multigenerational households like mine, cooperative and shared housing, and other forms of communal living. Shaping our homes to better address physical, social, emotional, and financial needs is essential for our survival, which many of the essays within explore. But *Living, Together* is also about how these forms of cohabitation don't always arise out of crisis; some people intentionally seek them out. They can be fun and flexible—a way of hacking adulthood, as contributor Rhaina Cohen writes about the home she shares with her husband and friends.

The fifteen essays and six Q&As in this anthology reflect a rich array of stories and perspectives. In fact, the only parameter I set is that contributors be currently based in the US, in order to show that communal living is happening right here, right now; it's not a distant phenomenon. You may bring assumptions to your reading—that this practice is mainly for the crunchy granola among us, that it predominantly takes place in rural areas, that it requires a specific spiritual or religious affiliation, or that an extended family member who resides with a nuclear family is a "freeloader," to name a few. But you'll quickly see upon opening *Living, Together* that all kinds of people live communally in all kinds of configurations and locations for all kinds of reasons.

Contributors range in age from their twenties to their nineties. They are diverse in gender, sexual orientation, race, class, and physical ability. While it's no surprise that some are writing about communal living in New York and California, others are writing about or from Vermont, Ohio, Illinois, Virginia, Georgia, Florida, South Dakota, Wyoming, Colorado, Arizona, Nevada, and Washington. There is one thing, however, that unites all of these people, from the first-time essayists to the authors with multiple books to their names: they've had the courage and commitment to pursue their most fulfilling and authentic lives through community. The choices they've made, which you'll hear about firsthand, have expanded our collective sense of what's possible.

The anthology unfolds in three sections: "Family Homes" tells the stories of households centered on family, biological and chosen, "Intentional Communities" focuses on housing arrangements built on shared goals and values, and "Beyond Housing" features perspectives of those who can't or don't want to live communally but are finding other forms of meaningful connection and mutual care. Together, these sections encourage us to broaden our definitions of family, home, and community.

One core question runs through the entire book: How might we live together in order to have happier, healthier, and more connected lives? Contributors unpack this, as well as related ideas, throughout the three sections. In "Family Homes," they wonder if there could be a sense of possibility and liberation around familial living arrangements that are unusual or even shameful in our culture. They contemplate the ways that capitalism, ableism, white supremacy, classism, heterosexism, and nationalism are rooted in our cultural assumptions around living with our families of origin as adults. This section asks whether doing so can heal childhood wounds, perhaps moving relationships forward in surprising directions. It encourages readers to look beyond their own personal histories—to other families, cultures, and even species—for alternative ways of forming home and community.

"Intentional Communities" invites readers to think about what it looks like to create homes around joint values and goals, including friendship, money, artistic community, nature, religion, cultural tradition, safety, help with child-rearing, and companionship in old age. Here, some contributors search for incremental ways of bringing community into their lives. Others meditate on the positive impact of communal living structures that were temporary by design. This section investigates whether communal living can ultimately give us the freedom to make choices that redefine our relationships to work, money, and the people around us. Are the challenges and hard work worth the freedom and joy? And are there particular groups who might benefit the most from communal living, such as young adults, retirees, those who identify as LGBTQ+, and religious and ethnic minorities?

Expanding on this last question, "Beyond Housing" asks readers to consider what building a communal *life* looks like, including how we can put stronger community-oriented systems in place outside of housing for specific groups of people. I hope every reader can see a piece of themselves in this third act. Through stories of developing close relationships with neighbors, forming identity-based groups and mutual aid organizations, hosting recurring dinner parties, and building chosen families, this section examines how even when communal living isn't practical—or desired—we can still discover ways to nurture and be nurtured by the people around us.

These pieces illustrate what we have to gain, individually and as a society, by returning to more localized forms of community and care, choosing to meet regularly within our communities rather than spending so much time alone scrolling on our phones. "Beyond Housing" interrogates whether people can truly stand in when systems fail us, such as during the AIDS crisis or COVID-19 pandemic, or when a deployment leaves a military spouse alone in a new state. Additionally, it examines what's often overlooked when we think about community for older people, who may disproportionately experience illness, disability, or social isolation. What can any of us organize in our neighborhoods to ensure that the most vulnerable aren't left behind?

As I've been editing this book, I often think about what another anthology editor, Margot Kahn, once wrote about the form: "When we look for ways in which to understand the divergent perspectives of others, there's no better book form than the anthology. This is the town hall bound in pages, to be held, discussed and reflected upon."[3] My hope is that reading this collection of distinct minds, hearts, and experiences inspires you to challenge the assumptions we're raised and socialized with, and to lean into the radical joy and freedom that comes with reconsidering the ways we live together.

There are a great many forces putting pressure on us right now, from the skyrocketing cost of living and the lack of a substantial social safety net to the acceleration of climate change to the fact that healthcare in the US is tied to employment and traditional family structures. There's so much that needs rethinking if we're going to remain resilient in today's world. Why wouldn't we begin with an idea as basic, primal, and necessary as home, guided by those with unique experiences to share?

Whether you've picked up *Living, Together* because you're curious about how communal living works, because you've felt lonely and aren't sure what to do about it, or because you're already a diehard supporter, you'll find that this anthology is a starting point for something bigger: expanding personal, and ultimately societal, expectations around how we could live. The title, *Living, Together*, speaks to my wish for what the book can be. A spark to pause and question, to share and discuss, and to plan and act towards a future that isn't just "living" but is sustainable and resilient against whatever happens next.

—SAMANTHA PAIGE ROSEN
April 2025

LIVING,
TOGETHER

PART I

FAMILY HOMES

SURVIVAL OF THE CONNECTED

Elizabeth Hart Bergstrom

In nature, this kind of care is remarkable but not uncommon. And if we choose to, if we work at it, we could make it more common again in our human communities too.

My mother's Vermont garden is a colorful ecosystem of plants, animals, and other creatures who are often competing for food or trying to eat each other. The red fox chases the deer mouse, the bluebird catches a worm, an aphid chews on the hydrangea stems, and a ladybug comes along to eat the aphid. This fits the view of nature presented in my school textbooks, which oversimplified "survival of the fittest" and saw nature as a brutal, kill-or-be-killed sort of place. But when I look closer, watching through the window of my attic apartment above my parents' house, I see a surprising number of different creatures cooperating and living in close quarters together.

In the front yard, a bumblebee drinks nectar from a purple aster flower, a relationship that is good for both of them—the bee gets energy from the nectar, and the flower gets pollinated. This is an example of mutualism, two species interacting in a way that benefits both.[1] Bumblebees live together in social groups, with each member of the hive having its own specialized role.[2] They often build their nests in former mouse burrows.[3] Many animals and plants interact this way too, in what's called commensalism—one species benefits, without harming or helping the other.[4]

In the backyard, under the surface of the soil, the roots of the sugar maple trees live in close relationship with fungi. Most plants make connections with fungus in this way, and these networks allow a fascinating form of cooperation.[5] Usually, this communal living benefits both the plant and the fungus: the tree gives some of its nutrients from photosynthesis to feed the fungus, while the fungus absorbs water and nutrients from the soil and shares them with the tree.[6] These networks also connect trees to each other to share resources and communicate across species and distance.[7]

Not far uphill from the backyard is the edge of a forest, where I hear ravens calling. These birds are some of the smartest animals around. Their intelligence and sociability mean they sometimes steal from each other, but they also cooperate with and comfort one another.[8] I've read about ravens playing games with other animals such as otters and gray wolves.[9] For their part, wolves are animals with complex social lives who take care of sick or injured packmates.[10]

Tonight, my sister's family walks from their house across the street for Sunday dinner. On my parents' screen porch, we set up a long folding table and load it with vinaigrette potato salad, bread from a local bakery, caprese salad, and platters of stuffed grape leaves, artichoke hearts, and vegetarian sausages. My sister grew the fingerling potatoes and tomatoes in her garden. The seven of us pull up chairs and pour glasses of cold limeade.

My niece tells us about her latest theater audition, my nephew shares how he just drove a car for the first time, and my sister explains her butterfly photography project. My brother-in-law describes swimming a mile in the Atlantic for a friend's seventy-fifth birthday. My teenage niblings have just watched *The Matrix* for the first time, so I ask excitedly if anyone else has seen *Point Break*, a 1991 cult classic about surfing bank robbers and the homoerotic tension between Keanu Reeves and Patrick Swayze. Sadly, they haven't.

The air is mild and soft. My parents' goldendoodle naps quietly under the table. Crickets chirp from the late August garden that blooms with white hydrangeas, pink cosmos, anemone flowers, and purple anise hyssop. We chat until dark, then go our separate ways—me to feed my two cats in the attic apartment, my sister's family to care for their black Lab and leopard geckos and shut their chickens safely into the coop for the night. The hens lay enough eggs for both households to make French toast and omelets, while they get plenty of cracked corn to eat and a coop to sleep in.

Where do I fit into this interconnected family ecosystem? It definitely wasn't my plan to be living in the same house as my parents the year I turned forty. I landed here six years ago when I became too sick to work or to live on my own.

Until my mid-thirties, I lived in and around New York and DC, worked for several nonprofits, fell in and out of several romantic relationships, and carted my cats, books, and bicycle to a new home every year or two. I visited my family at Christmas and for an occasional birthday or summer solstice. My brother, too, chose the city life, moving to Seattle.

My sister, on the other hand, chose the small-town life, and my parents retired to a house across the street from her a decade ago. Their Vermont family collective was lovely to visit, but the quiet made me nervous at the time. Their town—now my town too—has fewer than five hundred people, with one grocery market, one post office that doesn't deliver to our house, one burger joint, and one community arts nonprofit. By Vermont standards, we're not too rural because we live on a paved road that's close to everything we need. A slightly bigger town ten minutes away provides the coffee shops, independent bookstores, pharmacies, gas stations, and library I rely on.

My life now looks almost completely opposite to my life in Brooklyn in my thirties. Back then, I'd just finished grad school, two busy years that were bookended by a spine injury from a car crash, and then a broken arm and messed-up shoulder from a bike crash. School and work meant I had little time to recover from either. Five days a week, I took two subway lines to a sunny office in the West Village doing environmental writing that I thought was my dream job. In reality, it was stressful and exhausting being pulled in different directions by departments with conflicting priorities.

My apartment had a ton of space by New York standards, and my roommate was great, but we had a nest of roaches living in the dishwasher, rats running through the pipes, and a chronic water leak that made mushrooms grow from the ceiling. Sirens and traffic and motorbikes meant I never slept well. I loved going to Shakespeare in the Park, eating pizza and banh mi, wandering through art museums and bookstores, and going on dates in Central Park in spring and Coney Island in summer. It was a romantic, emotionally turbulent era of my life. The whole time, my body continued to break down, and my daily life was becoming more and more physically painful.

I'd had headaches, stomachaches, and depression since childhood, but my health went downhill so much that I was throwing up from migraines and nausea, collapsing on subway platforms from fatigue and dizziness, struggling to breathe from air pollution and asthma, and coping with chronic pain as routine as my morning coffee (which I eventually had to give up because of stomachaches and heart palpitations). Some days, painful eye infections blurred my vision.

In the course of a few years, I changed from being someone who biked fifty miles in a day, loved rock climbing, and hiked ten miles in the snow to someone who struggled to walk the few blocks from my apartment to the subway. My mind was a blur of pain and exhaustion. I couldn't stay awake or focus on my work. I could barely climb the single flight of stairs to my apartment, holding on to the banisters and then the walls with all the strength left in my hands. After wearing off the end of my umbrella from leaning on it to walk, I bought my first cane.

I scheduled appointments and got endless tests from medical specialists whose condescension made me feel as small as an ant. My primary care doctor said, "Your problems are psychosomatic." A rheumatologist said, "Just try swimming." A neurologist saw me struggling to stand up with a cane and said, "You're a young, healthy woman with your whole life ahead of you. It would be a shame to walk around with that *thing* in your hand if you don't have to."

Finally, a gastroenterologist made a diagnosis of an autoimmune illness that explained symptoms I'd had for almost fifteen years. I got the news in his office on West Twentieth Street on a dreary January day, and afterward, I sobbed on a bench outside. The diagnosis came too late for me to remain in New York. I'd used up all my sick leave, then my vacation time, and all the favors I was able or willing to ask from friends and significant others. Finally, I asked permission from my job to work remotely while staying with family in Vermont to recuperate, but they said no.

So, I took a medical leave. Just before Halloween, after the orange leaves had fallen to the ground, my two cats and I came to stay in the attic of my parents' blue Victorian house. Scattered around my few suitcases were bins of Christmas decorations, extra dishes and linens, my mother's sewing machine, and toys my niece and nephew had grown out of, like their stuffed rocking horse Gigi. I slept on a futon, having left my bed and other furniture in my Brooklyn apartment.

When it took more than a few months to start feeling better, I lost my job. It left a bitter taste in my mouth to write the resignation letter, knowing my boss had been allowed to work remotely for years. I sold or gave away almost all my furniture, my family and friends and partner helped pack up the rest of my stuff, and my dad rented a U-Haul and drove it five hours up to Vermont.

A few months later, I also lost my romantic partner when our long-distance relationship became too difficult and they didn't want to move. We'd been together for three years. Although it was a mutual decision, when we broke up over the phone on our anniversary, it felt like I'd been kicked while I was down.

Then came several years of having little space in my life for anything except trying to improve my health. I started using the word *disabled* to describe myself. I realized that becoming disabled is something that happens to all of us if we live long enough, and I worked on accepting the fact that it happened to me in my thirties. For years, I subconsciously believed that getting chronically ill must have been my fault. Psychologists call this the "just-world hypothesis"—the cognitive bias that bad things happen to bad people and good things happen to good people.[11] It's a tempting fallacy because it gives us some sense of control over our uncontrollable lives. I know now that there's nothing I did wrong to become sick, and there's nothing shameful about being sick or disabled.

During those years, I couldn't get out of bed on many or most days. My brain would send insistent messages to my arms and legs to move, to pull myself up to a sitting position using the futon armrest, but I could barely wiggle my fingers. A gray fog filled my head, and there was a crushing heaviness in every fiber of my muscles and bones. It was difficult to untangle how much of this weight was the severe fatigue that doctors still couldn't explain, and how much of it was depression, loneliness, and grieving for the life I'd once had.

Then came a global pandemic. Since I take medicine that suppresses my immune system, I barely left the house for a year or two. During that time, I felt terrified but sometimes less alone than before, because writing workshops and game nights became accessible to me when they moved onto Zoom.

It also helped that my family took care of each other in creative ways through the crisis. We each found new hobbies and routines we desperately latched onto—my mom watched *The Great British Baking Show* and baked loaf after loaf of sourdough, my dad started a weekly Zoom call with his four sisters from as far away as Denmark, and I got into jigsaw puzzles and writing postcards to voters. My sister took up butterfly-watching. When we got stir-crazy, we organized family movie nights. After arguing over what movie to watch, we ordered all kinds of candy from curbside grocery pickup, decorated a cardboard concession stand, and sold each other snacks for a dollar apiece, with the money going to our local food bank and other nonprofits.

Two years into the pandemic, another piece of the mystery illness puzzle fell into place when a doctor prescribed me medication for fibromyalgia. I had asked doctors about it years before, but they'd said dismissively, "You're not in enough pain to have fibromyalgia." The effectiveness of the medicine said otherwise, and little by little, the heavy gray fog lifted.

Now, I can't exactly say that I've miraculously recovered—some illnesses are likely to stay with me for the rest of my life. I manage them with a combination of pills, shots, and changes to how I eat, sleep, and move through the world. Just in the last year, these treatments have helped enough that I've been able to start to clear my head and put down a few roots, like the stewartia tree I planted with my family in the garden.

I don't know how I would have weathered this if it weren't for being able to live with family. I'm fortunate that my parents' house not only had space for me and my two cats but also an attic that had already been renovated by the prior owner with its own bathroom and kitchen. The attic doesn't have a separate entrance, and in practice, my life is very intertwined with that of my family. My parents and I eat dinner together and then watch TV in the evenings—recently lentil soup followed by *Only Murders in the Building.*

We share groceries and streaming subscriptions; my dad and brother-in-law share one electric lawn mower. My sister and I launched a business together, writing and editing and building websites for small businesses and nonprofits. I dress up for Halloween with my niece and nephew. I love being an aunt and getting to have long, rambling conversations with my family members.

We feed each other's pets and get the mail and pick the tomatoes when someone goes out of town. When we run out of eggs, my sister sends over a dozen from her chickens. When someone gets sick, we drop off medicine or soup and bread. I drive my sister on errands when her car is in the shop, my dad picks up my prescriptions and remembers when our cars need an oil change, my mom bakes and washes the windows and orchestrates holiday magic, and my brother-in-law knocks the snow off the roof for my parents, who are now in their seventies.

I'm still trying to figure out how to get back into a routine of housework and grocery shopping given my unpredictable fatigue. I still feel guilt and shame when I fear that I'm not "pulling my weight" or "being a productive member of society" or any of these kinds of ideas that I know are tangled up with capitalism and ableism.

I feel the desire for this to be a mutualistic community. I really want to be helpful, particularly as my parents get older. But I'm only well enough to work part-time, and only in a freelance business where my schedule can be flexible. I still have trouble with fatigue, needing to nap for several hours each day. I pay my parents for food and housing, though substantially less than market-value rent. Right now, in this family ecosystem, I'm like a bumblebee hibernating in a mouse burrow, borrowing space from someone else. Maybe that's all right.

Many days, I don't need a cane anymore. Some days, I do. I still lean on the banisters on either side of the stairs to help pull myself up the two flights to the attic. The banisters were installed to help my grandfather when he lived here briefly, before he moved to assisted living. The same with the sandpaper treads on each step that keep my feet from slipping, the grab bars in the shower, and the shower chair.

Sometimes my legs give out and I have to crawl across the room. I realized how bad it could have been if I'd been living alone when I had a severe reaction to a medication a few years ago. After being violently ill all night, I was lying on the floor unable to stand or speak until family members called 911. The paramedics had to rig up a mechanism to move me on a gurney down two flights of steep, narrow stairs to reach the ambulance.

I have a tremendous amount to be grateful for. I also don't want to claim that communal living in a multigenerational family is easy or necessarily idyllic. Many people I know don't have family that's emotionally supportive of them, or even still living. Even if they do, their families may not have room in their homes or budgets for them to move in.

Among the seven of us, there are conflicts and personalities and schedules to manage, and there is some communication that goes sideways. My parents and I argue about how to load the dishwasher, what temperature to set the thermostat, whether one of us is getting distracted while driving, how cranky I get from migraines and hypersensitivity to noise, and which megacorporations we should avoid buying from.

It helps that my immediate family shares a lot of interests and values. I'm not a black sheep here for being a vegetarian, atheist, pagan, Unitarian Universalist, queer writer. In fact, that's pretty ordinary in my family. All of us are artists, writers, musicians, actors, or scientists and science teachers. All of us are vegetarian or pescatarian. All of us have some connection to Unitarian Universalism (a nondenominational religion based on principles of justice, compassion, and an individual search for truth and meaning). And we've all gone together to rallies for progressive political candidates and reproductive rights. Although our experiences and symptoms are different, several of my family members have autoimmune illnesses too.

I feel generally comfortable being out to my family as a queer person. I've dated some since moving here, though my love life and the weirder, more independent parts of myself are hard to keep sight of while living so closely with family.

My idea of family is bigger than just biological or romantic ties, however, and I've worked on cultivating closer friendships in the last few years. I'm deeply grateful for friends who listen, adapt, and show compassion about my unpredictable health. In return, I do my best to support them when they cope with their own physical and mental health challenges. I've been reading about other animals that help each other whether or not they're related. Red foxes take care of kits who aren't always kin, and geese adopt unrelated goslings.[12] Scientists have found that mice will altruistically work to free another mouse from confinement, even if the two animals are strangers.[13]

In nature, this kind of care is remarkable but not uncommon. And if we choose to, if we work at it, we could make it more common again in our human communities too.

Our lives and communities aren't just about transactions, as much as our economic system tries to make it seem that way. Our worth isn't only in what we do—the work we complete, the societal expectations we meet, or the art we create. These days I aspire to be a true friend, good company, a kind human being, a better writer than I was yesterday, and part of a collective of family, friends, and the broader community. My goals in life are to experience more justice and more joy, and to help build a world where we can all experience those things. The shape of what that might look like is up to us.

YOU AND I WERE ROOMMATES ONCE

Adam Vitcavage

We were able to stop wearing masks in our own homes, maybe for the first time. Maybe in the way that only siblings can.

You and I lived together for the first fourteen years of my life in a shoebox house in urban Pennsylvania and then in an Arizona ranch surrounded by cacti. In the winter, we spread out a giant blue comforter on the living room floor, stepped into our bathing suits, and pretended to swim. You dressed me up in gowns when we played with Barbies. You terrorized me with a plastic Jabba the Hutt that made creepy sounds while I hid around corners. We had shoving matches at the top of the stairs. We never liked each other growing up and fought more than I think most siblings do. You were relaxed while I was uptight. I had a naturally short fuse, and you knew how to light it. Once I grew taller than you and developed a temper, our relationship became even more volatile. Beyond disagreements over who controlled the TV and your teasing me about my bowl cut, there were punches thrown, psychological warfare conducted, and items destroyed. When you left for college, I thought we'd never see each other outside of family gatherings.

Eleven years later, you called to say you were getting divorced and needed a roommate. You had lived with your ex in the suburbs and he handled everything. Your entire world orbited a life that you, at nearly thirty, were trying to leave. You didn't have any money saved. You had never seen a bill. You didn't know how to set up a new cell phone plan or get insurance. While your peers had done all of this a decade earlier, you were embarking on it all for the first time.

You downplayed the fact that you needed my help, and let me assume that I was just one of many roommate options. Years later, you told me that you didn't trust anybody else. No matter how much we fought as kids or teenagers, you felt safe with me, your know-it-all twenty-five-year-old brother who would still rather take a swing than talk about his feelings. Battling anxiety and depression, I was skilled at pushing people away. But you asked, so I agreed.

When we decided to become roommates, I didn't know that so much of who I am now would be shaped by how we grew up together—not as kids under Dad and Mom's roof, but as adults in a series of generic Phoenix apartments with beige carpets and off-white walls. At the time, our arrangement seemed convenient; looking back, I see it was more than that. You needed me, and I needed you.

At first, we lived parallel lives. I was an early bird and you were a night owl. I was a bookworm and you were a party girl. You swore that if we weren't related, you would never have chosen to spend time with me. But over years and tiny moments, we discovered that beneath our surface descriptors, we were both just seeking a place we belonged.

Together we worked on budgeting and bills. I helped you set up accounts you never had to create before, and you showed me how to cook and clean properly. We started going to concerts together and trying out new restaurants. We spent hours every week bonding over a shared love of trashing reality TV stars.

Living with you, I was able to be more than the typical considerate roommate—I was able to be myself. With previous roommates in college and early adulthood, there was a sense of masquerade. Not with us. If you wanted to play video games for sixteen hours or if I wanted to eat halushki for dinner five nights a week, that was okay. We were able to stop wearing masks in our own homes, maybe for the first time. Maybe in the way that only siblings can.

In the four years we were roommates, I learned a lot about how to be a human. You taught me that if I didn't improve at regulating my emotions, I would end up pushing everyone away. You didn't let me steamroll decisions and conversations. Most people would have dealt with my inflexibility and temper for a year and moved out after the lease ended, but you stuck around and forced me to breathe, listen, and bend.

While you learned to pay bills and manage a budget, there was more to it than that. After leaving a relationship that had dominated your entire adult life, you figured out how to trust people again.

You would think that after all of this, we'd stay in better touch, but once we didn't share a living room and I moved to Denver with my fiancée, we talked much less often. Both of us are "out of sight, out of mind" kind of people who keep to small social circles. Sure, we text memes and TV show recommendations, and comment on each other's travel pictures, but we rarely pick up the phone just to say *Hey, how are you doing?*

A few weeks ago, I gave you a call and we swapped updates. We were both thrilled to leave dead-end jobs. You found a new community you feel safe in. I'm happily married and own a house. You're in a new relationship, the healthiest you've ever had. My website and podcast continue to expand. Your dog, Beastie, is recovering after a health scare. Of course, we also chatted about *RuPaul's Drag Race* and *Vanderpump Rules*, hiking through the desert, and catching bands in dive bars. We even argued over which Thai restaurant we should go to on my next visit to Phoenix—we're still siblings, after all.

In 2014, you asked me to be your roommate because I was your little brother and you didn't feel like you had anyone else. I said yes because you were my sister, and why not? It couldn't be worse than living with frat bros I found on Craigslist. When we went our separate ways, in 2018, we'd grown into adults. And whether we talk once a day or once a week or once a month, I know you'll always be there on the other end of the phone because we're more than former roommates, more than even siblings. We're finally friends.

Q&A *with* JONATHAN ESCOFFERY

My father and mother taught me about community in their own distinct ways. They showed me how community was sustained through shared culture, mutual benefit, and consistently showing up for one another.

The child of Jamaican immigrants, Jonathan Escoffery grew up in Texas and Florida, first in the homes of family and friends who opened their doors to the new arrivals, and later, in his parents' townhouse in Miami, where they often hosted loved ones who followed them to the United States. When Hurricane Andrew destroyed their house, Jonathan and his family spent about a year sharing housing with extended family who had also lost their homes during the hurricane.

These early living experiences were some of many ways that the Escoffery family provided and received community support. Over the years, Jonathan watched his father eagerly sharing with friends and neighbors the produce he grew and his mother and aunts collectively saving money in a system that allowed contributors to draw a larger sum from time to time. All of this shaped his perspective on community, which has continued to evolve in his adult life.

Now in his forties, Jonathan belongs to a handful of communities: Californians, third-culture kids, second-generation immigrants, Jamaicans in America, Ridge Rats—people who grew up in Cutler Ridge, Florida—and fiction writers. His debut short story collection, *If I Survive You,* was published in 2022, and he founded a community called Boston Writers of Color in response to the centering of white writers in literary spaces. We spoke about what his experience as a first-generation American taught him about community, and the rewards and challenges of creating and participating in groups dedicated to the arts.

How and from whom did you learn about community?

My father and mother taught me about community in their own distinct ways, but one illustrative combined lesson was when they'd have me help gather clothes and other goods to fill barrels to send down to Jamaica, a practice most Caribbean people will recognize. We'd periodically send them to friends and family, and sent more in times of national disaster, such as when Hurricane Gilbert caused massive destruction in Jamaica. This taught me a sense of connection and responsibility to people who would have otherwise likely been out of sight and out of mind.

My mother was one of eleven children and many of her sisters wound up in Miami over the years. Growing up, they were often sharing and trading household goods and groceries, and participated in a "partner," a trust-dependent system of saving, lending, and borrowing money that might allow them to make bigger purchases when their "draw" date arrived.

My father was big on growing peppers and what fruits he could—bananas, sugarcane, coconuts, ackee—in his garden, and took pride in being able to share them with his friends, and they would do so in turn. He also frequented the Jamaican bars and restaurants that operated out of people's homes, presumably without license, and I'd accompany him. I saw how community was sustained through shared culture, mutual benefit, and consistently showing up for one another.

What was your experience of community between neighboring immigrant families?

Our neighborhood was ethnically and racially mixed, and I couldn't say which families were as newly arrived to the US as my family, though certainly many were first-generation immigrants. My older brother and I got to know our neighbors primarily through the kids who wandered out into the streets to play with us. Everyone was welcome and there were a lot of us on any given afternoon. This was the '80s, so kids were allowed to run loose for hours at a time unsupervised. I was also at an age where I had yet to understand much about cultural divisions, except that I knew we were Jamaicans and that most of the people around us weren't. When we'd inevitably wander into each other's homes, someone might comment on the "strangeness" of a dish our parents might have warming on the stovetop and that, more than anything, alerted us of our cultural difference.

Later, of course, cultural divisions began playing a more significant role in how my family and I moved through the city. From my teenage years, I noticed how much I participated in seeking out spaces that upheld and prioritized the shared values of people from the Anglophone Caribbean—the Jamaicans and Trinidadians and Guyanese and Virgin Islanders, and so on—be it through seeking out our food or music or general understanding of one another's humanity. For my parents, this may have been about recreating the communities they had before coming to the US, but for me, I know some of this was a reaction to the overt anti-Black racism I experienced in school, from non-Black immigrants and white Americans.

Do you think that broadening our conception of what housing can look like by turning away from single-family households, as well as leaning more into community, could address some of the challenges we face with the loneliness epidemic, the housing crisis, an aging population, and the climate crisis?

One tragic thing that happens when immigrants begin to assimilate into American culture is that some adopt the practice of putting their kids out of their homes—without any assistance—as soon as they're legally adults, or else as they graduate college. As a logical consequence, elderly parents are put in nursing homes and the like by adult children, who don't feel especially obligated to take care of them through to their last days. In many—or most—countries, both of these practices would be seen as unconscionable and I think there's much that could be gained by keeping multiple generations of a family together, without the shame American culture places on adult children, especially men, who live with their parents. In theory, that would add some amount of relief to the housing crisis, the loneliness epidemic, and a family's carbon footprint, and would allow for more support if and when adult children have children of their own.

Your debut short story collection, If I Survive You, *examines the survival and belonging of an immigrant family. Do you feel that community has helped you survive, whether in childhood or adulthood?*

I've already mentioned my need to find spaces that uplifted my sense of self-worth in my younger years, and those were largely in Caribbean spaces in Miami. Beyond that, literary spaces have done a lot for my mental health and material wealth. There's an associated cost with engaging in, and building, community, though. As an introvert, most social interactions, even very enjoyable ones, take a toll and require significant recouperation time. As a racial and ethnic minority, there's the constant hits to your psyche in having to fight not to be erased by the dominant white literary culture that's now decided it's the victim of largely failed attempts at making publishing more equitable. And then there's the responsibility you take on in helping to sustain a community; the emails and DMs and requests for free labor never stop.

Tell me about the times when you've lived communally as an adult.

I once managed a writing retreat in Western Massachusetts, and during that time, I lived with a rotating group of writers in residence. It began as a one-year fellowship and evolved into a two-year job that allowed me the time to get my first book finished. Week by week, I'd meet the most lovely, interesting, and sometimes accomplished people, and I met a few not-so-lovely people as well. I learned a lot about what I could reasonably ask of people to keep our communal space conducive for creating focused work. I learned a lot about boundaries too. Is a resident entitled to snore in his sleep, when the resident next door is a light sleeper, for instance? I learned that repeating your book's elevator pitch to five different residents 104 weeks in a row is a soul-crushing practice.

Did intentionally living in community feel different than living in community out of economic necessity?

The living arrangement was still out of economic necessity, until it wasn't, meaning it lasted until I'd saved enough money and had the next gig lined up. What felt intentional though, was that I was living with people who were, for the most part, committed to the common good of putting dedicated time toward our writing, the thing most of us valued more than anything.

How did your background and experiences prepare you to be part of these literary communities, and how do they inform the way you've gone on to build literary community?

Jamaicans tend to be fiercely bullheaded and individualistic in thinking, and being raised this way seems to have shielded me from assuming I'll be shut out of publishing or related academic spaces, even when these institutions have historically been unfriendly to Black people. It's usually after I've already broken into a space that I notice how truly bad it is. That tends to be when I make a decision about whether I can help improve a community, or if it's simply not for me. I went about forming Boston Writers of Color by seeking out and speaking to writers who shared my concern that GrubStreet's classes weren't as welcoming to writers of color as they should be. We held multiple town halls and instructor trainings, and worked for years to make things better.

What have you observed about the intersection of community and identity and belonging, whether racial, cultural, religious, artistic, or otherwise?

I think we all want to be seen, understood, and embraced for who we are, and that's already a difficult thing for a semi-aware artist type to feel, even in the confines of a homogenous community. Add any other element of difference in one's identity and things typically grow more challenging. But I think there's beauty in celebrating our differences, and there's no better place to do it than in the arts.

RENOVATIONS AND REBIRTHS

Dani McClain

> *I have gotten to watch the woman who guided me as I learned to walk, talk, feed myself, and venture out of the house on excursions learn again how to do these things herself.*

The house where I grew up had been my mom's childhood home before it was mine, the place where my maternal grandparents raised their eight daughters. I had lived with my mother in apartments in Cincinnati before moving as a toddler to the ranch home in Camp Dennison, a community of a few hundred people located northeast of the city. Built in 1928 by my grandfather's maternal grandparents, the four-bedroom, two-bathroom house had always felt like home, even when it was a destination for weekend overnights and holiday parties. My aunts, uncles, cousins, other extended family, and neighborhood kin had gathered there long before I was born.

When I was eight, my Aunt Pam joined us. My grandmother had recently died at fifty-eight from lung cancer and my grandfather had been gone five years, killed at barely sixty by a heart attack. The grief surrounding their early deaths hung heavy in the rooms I shared with my mother. When my aunt came, she brought with her a lightness, a sense of possibility. Together, she and my mom set about the work of creating an updated, contemporary version of the house that reflected who they were and aspired to be as women in their thirties. They painted the spacious front room and dining room in a pale lemon yellow and put down similarly colored rugs, choices that reflected a sleek sophistication and their relentless commitment to spotlessness. They bought new furniture, including a white couch, for the living room and painted its brick fireplace white, further elevating the space from its cozy but lived-in feel. One of the four bedrooms was transformed into a family room with a cream-colored tiled floor, a wall of windows, and a skylight. Off that sunroom they built a deck overlooking the spacious backyard and in-ground pool. Two single professional Black women invested their time and money in their family home, and in doing so achieved a Black elegance much like what the Huxtables brought to the TV world every Thursday night. And they accomplished it all without a husband in sight.

This was the two-parent family with whom I lived until I was eighteen, and who I claimed as my innermost unit of blood relations until my aunt's death in 2015. Growing up in a house with two women at the head shielded me from a patriarchal domestic framework and provided me with a different model for adulthood and family making. I remember very little tension in that home. There were no displays of domination, only expressions of sharing power. The culture was collaborative, respectful, and kind. I learned over the course of that decade how two people can join efforts to create a refuge for themselves and each other. They did yard work together, planting flowers and mowing the lawn in the warm months, and raking leaves and shoveling snow when the temperature dropped. They cleared the gutters when it was time to ready the house for winter. They vacuumed the pool, vacuumed the floors, dusted, cooked. Domestic work wasn't gendered. I picked up some chores as I got older, but mostly I was encouraged to focus on my schoolwork and the extracurriculars I got involved with over those years. I knew I could expect to see my mom and aunt at my soccer games and track meets, the school plays and awards ceremonies. I never lacked the assurance of their love and support.

Twenty-five years after departing this often-idyllic childhood home for college, I came to know it in a new and different light. Late in the morning of January 12, 2021, I picked up my daughter from preschool and drove her the half hour from central Cincinnati to that house in the suburbs, as I did most weekdays. When I arrived, I found my youthful and athletic sixty-seven-year-old mother collapsed on the floor of her bedroom, unresponsive. The paramedics took her to the nearest hospital, and it was there I learned she had suffered a brain bleed and would need to be airlifted elsewhere for an emergency surgery to relieve the pressure in her skull. It was not clear during these fear-filled hours whether she would survive the operation. She did.

Thus began the long road of my mother's recovery from a hemorrhagic stroke that nearly claimed her life. She would stay in the neuro ICU for just shy of two weeks and then move to an inpatient rehabilitation program for almost a month. In those frigid January and February weeks, I shuttled between the apartment where I lived with my child and those rooms where my mother mostly slept, suspended somewhere between this world and the next. I made the commute between my home and her temporary homes, places where first a ventilator aided her labored breathing and then where she began the arduous tasks of learning again how to speak and how to move through the world without full use of her left limbs.

On February 19, my mother went home. Or, I should say, she came home to my daughter and me. In the weeks following her stroke, I made arrangements to move from our apartment into her house, where she'd lived by herself since my aunt's death. The lightning-fast consolidation of two households into one was chaotic and grueling. It could not have happened without the support of family and friends near and far who packed and moved boxes, organized and brought meals, provided childcare, and gave of their time and resources in ways I still haven't understood how to properly acknowledge. Perhaps there is no appropriate expression of gratitude. But I now know that mutual aid is real. Selflessness is real. Community can be real, a set of actions, not just a buzzword. My mother, daughter, and I survived those winter months because we are loved, and that network of beloveds formed a circle of warmth and support around us while the winds of circumstance whipped about, threatening to undo us.

Once those winds died down a bit, there we were: three generations in a house that had held my family for three generations prior. It had provided refuge for my recent ancestors and now it would provide refuge for my mother, my daughter, and myself. Because the house is one level, it was accessible to my mother, who was confined to a wheelchair in those months before she learned how to walk with the help of an orthotic brace and quad cane. A carpenter friend and his architect father donated their time and built a wooden ramp to the front door, allowing my mother to bypass the several steps from ground level into the house. In addition to that external modification, we made small changes inside: Grab bars were installed in the bathroom and at the entryway to the sunken kitchen. My daughter's daybed, which had been my own as a child, was moved into a larger bedroom to allow more space for her to play. A display cabinet filled with antiques was emptied and transported out of the house to make room for my daughter's play kitchen. My mother had new required accessories as well. A bedside commode made using the toilet easier. I stored her shower chair in a corner of the smallest bedroom, which is where two of my mom's sisters stayed on and off during those first months as we struggled to find and orient to the new normal.

I decided not to sleep in that smallest bedroom, a choice I knew would not please my mother. For one thing, my aunts who stayed overnight to help were in their seventies and needed a comfortable place to rest. But there was another reason behind my decision. The three bedrooms were clumped together in the back of the house, and I felt strongly that when the day was finished, I needed as much space around me as possible. Once I had my daughter and my mom tucked comfortably in their beds, and I had cleaned the kitchen and taken care of whatever final tasks needed tending to, I needed to be alone with my thoughts and my TV shows and my phone calls and my scrolling. I was desperate for whatever privacy I could find in that hour or two or three before I went to sleep and then got up and did it all over again.

So when that same friend who also built the ramp agreed to help move my bed from my apartment to my mom's house, I had him assemble it in her living room. I took over that spacious front room—the jewel of the house that I'd watched my mom and aunt transform with its pristine lemon-yellow and the white brick fireplace over which hung a signed, original Gilbert Young graphite drawing. I moved into storage the white couch and the tchotchkes that had long lined the room's glass shelves. I made space for my queen-size bed, a desk, two bookshelves, my own photos and knickknacks, and a folding screen that did little to shield my makeshift bedroom from the sight line of anyone entering the front door. I didn't care. It was what I could do to create my own little apartment within this house to which I'd returned under less-than-ideal circumstances.

My mother and daughter resting on the other side of the house, my endless to-do list paused for the night, I could try to return to myself as a woman in her early forties, the me who had been a writer and thinker in the midst of what felt like a fulfilling career. If I needed to stay up late working or get up early to sit at my laptop, I could do so without fear of disturbing either of my charges and losing what little I could cobble together of the precious silence. I could return to myself as someone with friends I could call and a life outside these domestic and caregiving demands. I could peruse the apps and try to reclaim the me who wanted to date, or binge prestige or trash TV. I could dream of writing another book. I could simply catch my breath. I knew my mother hated that I'd taken over a room that she and her sister and their own mother before them had decorated with such pride. But I felt I deserved it. And so I enjoyed what little solitude I created there.

My mother's recovery remained at the center of our joint efforts, but other aspects of our lives were in progress. There were new routines and practices to establish, existing ones to tweak given the new environment. I was, after all, parenting a four-year-old. Making sure her life was filled with joyful, rich, and developmentally appropriate experiences was a priority as well. After six months in our new home, she started kindergarten. Overall, the transition seemed to be smooth for her. She'd had overnights and weekends at the house since she was a baby, and it had long been a second home to her, just as it had been for me before I moved in as a toddler.

I became mother to a school-age child just as my workload on the domestic front morphed into something new and significant. I had been the only adult in our rented two-bedroom walk-up since soon after my daughter's first birthday. Now I was the only able-bodied adult in a hundred-year-old house on a quarter acre lot. The house had many demands, including a raccoon that had nested in the attic for the winter, a significant plumbing issue, a washer/dryer that needed moving from the unfinished basement—which was only accessible from outside—to the ground level of the house. I'd grown up watching two people collaborating to take care of such things. Now, here I was mostly alone, although my friends were there to chip in when I called on them. One drove down from Yellow Springs to clear the gutters with me that first fall. I've had help raking leaves and shoveling and salting walkways. But it has largely been me, urging my mom toward decisions and marshaling forces, placing calls and managing plans.

That first year, friends would comment on how commendable I was, and I'd stare at them blankly, unsure what to say. I just did the next thing in front of me, the thing that had to be done. At forty-two, I felt firmly middle-aged but also too young to be faced with the challenges of caregiving. Two years after my mom's stroke, I read a *New York Times Magazine* article headlined "The Agony of Putting Your Life on Hold to Care for Your Parents" by Jaeah Lee.[1] The story echoed some of my experience and placed it in a broader context. In it I learned that my "sandwich generation" experience was less unique that I'd thought. In fact, "the share of caregivers who are under forty-five quintupled over the past two decades, to nearly 66 percent from 16 percent," Lee writes. Our boomer parents are living longer, but with more disabilities and less financial stability than their own parents.

Like me, the woman profiled in the article was a single mother living with her children and her father as she helped him recover after a traumatic event. Like me, her career felt tenuous as caregiving moved to take a central role in her life. Like me, she spent her days doling out medication, monitoring blood pressure, ferrying her dad to doctor's appointments, and peppering clinicians with questions. The article and its comments section, full of the testimonies of exhausted and overwhelmed caregivers, filled me with anxiety as I came to better understand the structural failures that shift the work of tending to ailing elders and disabled kin to family members. The health insurance system offers little support, and many of us can't afford professional caregivers, who are themselves underpaid and vulnerable to exploitation by employers. But reading the article also highlighted the ways I wasn't quite so bad off as the thirty-four-year-old Cleveland woman who had let the reporter peer into her family's life.

For one, my mother is a homeowner, and I moved in with her, not the other way around. In doing so, I stopped paying rent and utilities. I covered groceries and picked up other household expenses. Some of these have been significant, particularly in the early weeks and months when my mother was still convalescing, her brain too fragile to do much beyond repair itself. I also paid the aides who cared for my mom in those first years so that I could get time to work or otherwise be away from the house. It would be nice to receive pay for the caregiving I provide, and I know such an arrangement is possible in some circumstances. But I haven't pursued compensation. My mother and I have had a loving relationship, and I've felt it's been my duty to show up for her. Perhaps more importantly, the arrangement isn't ruining me financially, and I am likely breaking even. This adds to the feeling that my mother and I are supporting each other, a faint echo of the support I watched my aunt and her offer each other.

My daughter and mother were thick as thieves in those infant and toddler years before my mom's stroke, and I believe my daughter's presence has hastened my mother's recovery. I've seen it in the way my daughter has insisted on rambling, fast-paced conversations in spite of the aphasia that often makes my mother's words falter. My child is undeterred by the verbal stops and starts, motivated as ever to laugh and joke with her grandmother. I've seen the healing potential in the way they cuddle in my mom's bed, and I've watched my mother strive to gain more mobility so she can be present with my daughter. They can no longer go on lengthy walks, or take drives together, chase each other around the yard, or roll around on the floor. But even the ability to walk into my daughter's room, to sit beside her bed, and to read with her brings my mother joy. She is rarely so happy as when on the sidelines at my daughter's soccer games or in the audience at her dance recitals. As we near four years since that January day when everything changed, my mom can again care for my daughter while I'm out or otherwise engaged. I never expected we'd be here again.

This intimacy benefits not just them but me as well. While I am often hungry for privacy, I rarely suffer from loneliness or feelings of isolation. I enjoy the simple but comforting ritual of eating dinner together most nights, and the stress-reducing practice of sharing expenses. But the biggest benefit of living with my mom over these years has been that it's given me a front row seat as she's clawed her way back from the brink of death. I have gotten to watch the woman who guided me as I learned to walk, talk, feed myself, and venture out of the house on excursions learn again how to do these things herself. I have been given the opportunity to watch—and perhaps even midwife—a rebirth.

I understand that I am one of the lucky ones. For many caregivers, their loved one's health and well-being could be represented by a line that generally trends downward. My mother is aging, of course, and there will be more decline. But these past few years have also been marked by significant improvements. She has committed herself to physical, speech, and occupational therapy. Her words come more fluidly now, with less halting as she scans her mind for what she wants to say. She works tirelessly to build strength in her legs and improve her gait.

She is steadfast and determined, and has gained more independence than I thought possible. When my resentments run high, I remember this: I am learning to see the honor in providing care, understanding that it costs me relatively little to open that jar, retrieve that fallen object from the floor, sweep, rake, shovel, arrange the refrigerator so she can find what she needs—all things she would love nothing more than to be able to do on her own. She is and has been working doggedly at recovery. I help and observe and learn. Meanwhile, my daughter gets to grow up in a family that is rooted in collaboration, respect, and kindness, just as I did.

A POLYAMOROUS COMMITMENT

Alex Alberto

I was tempted to give up, to surrender to societal messages that monogamous nuclear families were more solid, more manageable.

When I broke up with the first partner I ever shared a home with, I decided I wanted to live alone, possibly forever. That decision may seem cynical for a twenty-four-year-old, but it was rooted in how stifled I felt as a traditional couple. The fact that my partner and I lived in a remote region of Eastern Canada, taught at the same school, and shared the same friends didn't help. My whole identity felt tied to one person. Plus, it bothered me that I experienced guilt for being attracted to a coworker or flirting with the barista at the coffee shop. I loved my partner, but my choices were to either stay with him and never experience romantic and physical intimacy with anyone else, or leave him for the idea of *everyone else*. I wanted a more open relationship model than the one society offered—and he did not.

After we split, I spiraled into an aching depression. It was different from my previous breakups; aside from the heartbreak, I started to believe I was fundamentally flawed, like there was something inherently wrong with me, because the conventional relationship model had never felt quite right. I was envious of those who appeared content in traditional monogamous partnerships, and I questioned why I couldn't find that same fulfillment. Was I afraid of commitment? Selfish? Bored too easily? Would I need to jump to a new relationship every time I hit the two-year mark? Compounding the turmoil, I was simultaneously grappling with my sexuality and gender identity. I wasn't straight, but I wasn't gay either. Girlhood and womanhood clashed with my inner sense of self, but I didn't know how or why. Everything seemed askew, like I was meant for something else, but I couldn't pinpoint what. It wasn't until I decided to experiment with polyamory that things began to snap into place.

My initial interest in non-monogamy stemmed from the desire to build multiple meaningful relationships with people I cared about, and to have the utmost independence in my romantic life and living space. I made that clear to my next partner, Don, whom I met after moving to New York City to study educational technology. Don had come to the East Coast from Alabama to study psychology, and conducted research on the trauma carried by survivors of heart attacks. He'd never thought about non-monogamy before reading my dating profile. But he was almost thirty-six and hadn't been truly happy in a relationship for more than a year at a time. He was willing to experiment.

Don and I quickly developed joint long-term goals, but we intentionally decided not to move in together. We wanted space for alone time and to see our other partners, so we spent three or four days a week together at his place and rented my studio apartment on Airbnb for short-term stays. On the days that we were together, we were intentionally *together*, rather than simply coexisting in the same space. It felt refreshing to commit to each other over and over without the gravity of a shared home. And when I hosted another partner, I could be solely focused on them—in *my* space, with *my* art on the walls, and *my* energy filling the room.

Yet as time went on, I wondered if living on my own would really fulfill me in the long term. As my experience with polyamory deepened, so did my interest in cohabitation. When Don started dating Bridget, the bond I developed with her was unlike anything I'd experienced before—a mix of friendship, fondness, intimacy, and trust that stemmed from our romantic love for the same human. Don and I celebrated New Year's Eve with Bridget and her other partner. I often went to her place for tea and tarot, and we confided in each other and held space for tears when we hit rough patches. When an apartment opened across the hall from mine, I found myself fantasizing about Bridget moving in. We could share leftovers, spontaneously watch movies in our sweats, and plant perennials in the empty raised beds at the front of the building.

While I still wanted some independence in my living situation, I began to develop a yearning to enmesh minute aspects of my daily life with multiple people. It's a common misconception that polyamory is only about individualistic, hedonistic needs. A way to have sex or casual dates outside of a primary relationship. For some, it is. But for me, it quickly became a way to build a new kind of family, one that keeps me free to be my whole self and gives me room to evolve. Polyamory had begun to make me more collectivist in every area of my life. It taught me how to share romantic love and sex, which culturally are the most dangerous things to share. Once I became comfortable doing that, sharing living space, schedules, daily life, and finances with more people didn't sound overwhelming or stifling anymore.

I never got to live across the hall from Bridget. But several years later, after she and Don broke up, Don and I bought a farmhouse in Upstate New York. After leaving my tech job to work on a farm for a season, I decided I wanted to start my own. Soon after, Aly, one of Don's partners, moved in part-time. Aly, a writer and musician, shared Don's Southern roots and my love of creative writing. The three of us all relied on each other for different things that we were individually good at and enjoyed: I was best working around the house, Aly at cooking, Don at budgeting and carrying the emotional labor of relationship check-ins. As we renovated the house, Aly helped me pull laminate flooring in the living room, revealing old wood planks beneath. Collaborating on house renovations often led Don and me to speak with irritation to one another, so we avoided it when we could. Don and Aly slept in the same bed, and I spent nights in mine with piles of books next to me, relieved that my preference for sleeping on my own did not leave anyone feeling lonely.

It was Aly who first gave shape and substance to my co-living dream, so when she decided that she no longer wanted to build a life with us Upstate, I was gutted. Just as I'd begun dreaming in earnest of a polyamorous family, it started to feel unattainable. It's not that everything was perfect with Aly. The months leading to our breakup had been draining and, of course, managing two people's needs and emotions was tougher than one. After she left, I did enjoy the calm, and the reduced frequency of delicate family check-ins.

I was tempted to give up, to surrender to societal messages that monogamous nuclear families were more solid, more manageable.

And it wasn't as if there were lines of polyamorous candidates beating down our door. So, how would we find others to join Don and me? It was hard enough for two people who had chemistry and aligned life goals to connect. Was hoping for three or more delusional?

But then I'd look back on the happy times we all shared at home with Aly, and how sharply those times contrasted with what my life had become since she left. When Don traveled for work, I was left alone to care for our chickens, our land, and our house. I missed writing sessions with Aly on the love seat in my reading nook. I missed our Saturday night check-ins over dinner, where the three of us set individual and family goals, discussed how we could support one another, and made space for anything we'd struggled with personally or as a unit. With just Don, I was part of a couple. With Aly, I was part of a *family*. I would never be able to grow that family if I gave up at the first setback; I needed to commit to the labor required to build something for which no blueprint existed.

The following winter, when our friends Hannah and Joe were in need of temporary housing for four months, we invited them to move in with us. It felt nice having them, and they helped to fill the void Aly left. Hannah had just learned that she was pregnant, and week by week, we would lay a seed or fruit that corresponded to the fetus's growth chart on our kitchen table, and look at it with wonder. First a poppy seed, then an apple seed, eventually a blueberry. When Hannah asked if I would speak French, my native language, to the baby, I was overcome with emotion—gratitude, belonging, love. Then Hannah asked me, unprompted, what her kid should call me. She normally would have thought Auntie or Uncle, but given my gender-queerness, she wanted to know if there was a term that would make me feel good. I began imagining their toddler calling me Zuntie. Even though our arrangement was temporary, as Hannah and Joe did not share our long-term co-living dreams, it gave me the opportunity to reconsider yet another decision I'd made in my early twenties—that I did not want kids.

I never possessed a biological clock. Not the one that was supposed to make me want "a family." Or at least not a nuclear one, the type of family that includes two adults who are exclusive romantic partners and a kid or three. In my mid-twenties, when I would say I didn't want kids, people would reply, *Oh you'll see, you're still young.* In my early thirties, they would say, *You can get pregnant in your forties nowadays.* The problem wasn't only that my uterus had always felt like a spare part crammed in my body by mistake. It wasn't even the shrieking cognitive dissonance at the thought of raising tiny humans on a planet that's increasingly ablaze. Fundamentally, it was that the visions of parenting I'd glimpsed seemed claustrophobic and unsustainable, with so much burden on two adults.

Growing more secure in my gender identity, and feeling the warmth of being a Zuntie to a new baby, I became increasingly attuned to the way that children could enter the life Don and I were building.

Now it feels like everything between that first adult break-up and the present was preparing me for Saga, who Don met on a dating app around the time Hannah and Joe moved out. Saga lived in New York City, a three-hour drive from our Upstate farmhouse and its surrounding acres, which could make getting together a challenge. Moreover, she didn't intend to move elsewhere anytime soon. On their first date, she told Don that, after living abroad for over a decade and moving back to the US as a single mom, it had been hard to get settled and find community again. But Don was clearly taken with her, so he made the effort. They fell in love. I would later hear that Saga's heart opened for him in part from the stories I'd written about Don, our love, and the life we were building.

Almost a year after Don and Saga started to date, while I was away on my book tour, Saga's mother had surgery. The recovery was much more difficult than they'd anticipated, and it put Saga into the role of caregiving for her two young kids and her mother on her own. She was overwhelmed, anxious, and exhausted. Don drove down to the city and spent a few days with them, while some of our friends looked after our chickens Upstate. He dropped off and picked up the children from school, Saga made food for everyone, they tag-teamed bedtime reading and house cleaning. Saga's mother was grateful that Don shuffled his schedule at the last minute to come.

When I returned from my tour, I was drained. I'd driven three thousand miles through the Midwest and hadn't had a single day off in weeks.

"I look at our system, and it doesn't work," I told Don, leaning on the kitchen counter while I waited for the kettle to boil. "It makes no sense that you had to drive three hours to go help, that Saga shares a bedroom with the kids in an apartment that is frigid in the winter, while we have all this room up here. We're getting farther away from our goals. Instead of combining resources, we're spreading them."

Don slid his chair back and crossed his legs, taking a sip of his cold brew.

I sighed, and continued: "I know that Saga's life is in the city, and I want to respect that, but it seems like she loves it up here so much. The kids do too."

Over the prior year, as they visited us Upstate more often, I found myself imagining what it might be like to be a significant caregiver for Saga's kids.

Don slowly put his mug down. "I know for a fact that if you told Saga that *you* would like her to live with us, she would be overjoyed."

This surprised and delighted me. I had understood that Saga's commitment to the city, the kids' school, and her community there was nonnegotiable. But I had already developed a deep affinity for Saga because she shared her inner world so easily. She read an advanced copy of my book and would often reach out to tell me how much she identified with specific passages. It made us develop emotional intimacy quickly—and realize we both aspired to the same style of polyamory.

"Saga's mom will go back to Sweden half the year when she retires," Don said. "That changes how anchored Saga is to the city. Plus, she didn't know that she could even dream of a family like this before meeting me, and you."

The next time the three of us were together, we did a whiteboarding session: If we dreamed big, what could our communal life look like? We listed characteristics of the ideal physical space, and envisioned our routines, responsibilities, and co-parenting roles. We also spent some time writing down our individual concerns, so we could get ahead of issues that might arise. Filling the whiteboard made our imminent move feel real. We were all ecstatic.

The first few months of cohabitation were a true honeymoon. The kids loved their new elementary school and made friends right away. Saga and I split the early weekday mornings getting the kids out of the door to the school bus, and Don, who is not a morning person, led dinner and homework in the evenings. After reading bedtime stories in the living room, Don and I each carried a kid to their bedroom, followed by Saga bringing their blankets and stuffed animals. Then the three of us adults lined up to give them goodnight kisses. The oldest always wanted a soft kiss on the forehead and requested one for her favorite stuffie too, and the youngest asked for a kiss on top of his head, while hiding his face under his covers and squealing with joy. Don and I turned Saga into an avid *Survivor* fan, and we binged old seasons together on the couch, rotating nightly who sat in the comfiest corner. We each naturally found tasks that we liked or didn't mind: Saga collected eggs from the chickens daily, I took care of garbage and recycling, and Don handled grocery shopping.

We made sure everyone got at least half a day of dedicated weekly rest time when they weren't working or on parenting duty.

While we thought that whiteboarding and planning before moving in would shield us from the biggest challenges, I wasn't prepared for how intense adapting to this new life would be. Parenting wasn't instinctive for me. I wanted to read the how-to books and discuss every situation that arose so we could all make empirically based decisions that would be best for the kids and the family. Saga, burnt out from years of being a single mom, found talking through parenting strategies and interventions draining and emotional, and she preferred to avoid it. And Don was much more intuitive and comfortable making parenting decisions on the fly. Our communication styles and habits didn't line up naturally either. I wanted weekly family check-ins so we could discuss our joys and struggles openly, but Saga had a hard time understanding her own emotions in this new family context. Talking about them was more difficult than she expected. So many of us come to polyamory after experiencing disappointments, betrayals, or broken trust in prior monogamous relationships, and Saga was no different. Learning to be vulnerable not only with a new partner but also with that partner's partner required time and patience. I had to demonstrate to Saga that I was trustworthy and committed to understanding her experience. Saga had to show me that she wanted me to take on a parental role and to feel like I belonged in the family structure she was building with Don and the kids.

All blended families go through a transition period in which everyone has to learn how to live together. But polyamorous families have more adults and more relationships, and most of us are navigating without well-honed instincts or established models to guide us. One of the biggest challenges for us was that the usual indicators of whether relationships are functioning well don't apply in the same way, especially for relationships between metamours—two people with a mutual partner. I didn't know when to defer to Saga and/or Don, and when to insist on a compromise. If Saga and Don were unbothered when the kids left the restroom without washing their hands, should the fact that everything in me said we should intervene to build a new habit prevail? If I could see fifteen small changes to our daily routine that would almost certainly make our home life calmer and more organized, was it appropriate for me to suggest a family meeting to discuss them? I believed these would help, but I also knew that proposing changes would feel like yet another demand on my partner and my metamour. Things got so challenging that I was tempted to give up, again. Maybe Don and I worked better as a separate pair, without co-parenting or building a home with Saga. Maybe this particular combination of people and circumstances was incompatible. Maybe it would be best to go back to the way Don and I used to live, spending only half the week together, with separate living spaces; he could have one with Saga and the kids, and one with me. And I could be more of a Zuntie to the kids, living nearby but not in the same house.

But we'd been living together for only six months. If our family was nuclear, like all the other families around me, would I give up that easily? If I was monogamously married and having relationship challenges exacerbated by two young kids, would my friends still tell me I should give up before truly giving it a fair try? Wouldn't they worry about what was best for the kids?

I'd been wanting a family like this for so long, and when we decided to all move in together, Don and I intentionally made a commitment to Saga and the kids. We were not "trying out" being parents. I reminded myself I had to stay devoted to the hard work it takes to build a family that resists societal norms, and I continued to work through our challenges.

Eventually, we had a breakthrough. Saga and I both realized that we needed to make changes, for ourselves, for each other, and for Don and the kids. We laid out our fear and anxiety, guilt and despair, and cried. We discovered that many of our fears were aligned; we were both terrified that we'd jumped into this new family too quickly and wondered whether our disparate communication styles and preferences signaled a fundamental incompatibility hard to overcome. We learned about important efforts the other was making to improve our life together.

I told Saga that the reason I scheduled myself to watch the kids when she was taking a break was that I had been trying to give her space and rest, not because I didn't want to be around her. I revealed I'd been seeing a parenting coach to build my confidence and to co-parent better. Saga shared that she had found a new therapist to work specifically on what was blocking her communication. Over time, we started communicating more effortlessly and regularly. Outside of scheduled family check-ins, I stopped hesitating before sending questions to our "nest" text thread. Saga began to wake up a little earlier to come hang out with me in the kitchen before Don woke up, which often resulted in spontaneous, vulnerable conversations.

Through trial and error, we figured out routines that allowed us to co-parent better and to make room for each of our particular styles, while also staying on the same page. I practiced relying a bit more on my intuition and living with some imperfections when it came to parenting. Don and Saga agreed to implement simple routines for the kids that ultimately made everyone feel better, like having them lay out their clothes for the next morning, and tidying up the playroom weekly. And we all prioritized handwashing! I anticipate we'll have more challenges over the years. And each time we have a breakthrough, we'll be reminded of the gleeful feeling of home that we have created together. The joy is euphoric because we've had to fight so hard to get to it. We know how rare and unique it is.

I was able to build the beautiful polyamorous home I have because I *committed* all the way through. I committed to not giving up on the dream of it when it didn't work out with Aly. I let myself enjoy cohabitation with Hannah and Joe even if they didn't want to live together long-term. And when I did find the right people, I committed to not giving up on them. To investing the same amount of effort into our family and relationships that people would expect of a traditional marriage. I committed to continually blocking out the messages we receive from popular culture that "normal" families are better. To not letting myself become worn down by having to explain our family over and over again to school administrators, colleagues, and other parents at the playground.

When monogamous folks have relationship difficulties, they ask themselves: *Is this a good fit? Am I showing up as the best partner I can be? Should I be expecting something different from my partner?* But when polyamorous folks encounter challenges co-living with partners and metamours, the first question we ask ourselves is: *Can this structure even work?* To find the strength to continually commit, we have to believe in the revolutionary idea of a polyamorous family—and acknowledge that we're trailblazers. This means most things will be harder for us. However, those difficulties don't necessarily reflect our family's compatibility, nor do they signal that we're making a mistake. They mean only that trailblazing itself is hard, and that the work of polyamorous family building—and talking about it—is necessary. They mean that we must have faith in a form of family we've never truly seen, and in the people who have taken that leap of faith with us.

COME WITH US

Hannah Grieco

When they offer to take the girls to school, say, "No, I've got it." Then stop. Say, "Actually, yes. Thank you." Say, "Thank you so much."

Scrub the black mold out of the cabinets and closets, muttering first about how your father should have taken care of this before the movers arrived and second about how you should have known the way your parents were living, should have realized on one of your visits, should have come over years earlier and deposited your three young children in their living room, like you always did, but instead of sitting there and complaining or leaving quickly, handing off diapers and art projects, instead you should have ordered pizza and listened to everyone play Uno while you emptied each cupboard plate by plate, stack by stack, and scoured the black surfaces.

Begin planning large meals, like a catering company. Begin ordering groceries. Begin cooking for seven, balancing the monotone tastes of your rigid children. Plain meat that never touches the green beans for the eleven-year-old. Toasted garlic bread that isn't too garlicky for the six-year-old. Weigh these with the creams and sauces that your parents have grown accustomed to eating at restaurants every night. There is a balance, hard to find. Watch the nine-year-old, the in-between daughter. She'll eat anything. She learned, years ago, how to walk any tightrope.

Shovel snow. Take the garbage cans to the curb. Do the dishes. Fix the washing machine. Grow exhausted from the extra work of so many inhabitants who need you to do so many things. Grow irritated with your mother's cheery, "Good morning!" from her side of the house. You already worked hard before this, and now there is more. There is much more.

Secretly take videos of your son playing chess with his grandfather at 10 a.m., home from school after spending the night in your arms, sobbing about wanting to die. "Checkmate!" he yells, then dances around the room, his stimming fingers fluttering. "Okay, okay. One more game," your father replies. This man who rarely speaks. This man who was not patient with you when you yelled or cried as a child. He has grown the ability to wait, to breathe, to whisper encouragement, to touch his grandson's arm and say, "No, there's nothing in the shadows." To say, "I'm right here. You're okay."

Take a nap. Wake up to knocking on your door, and then your mother's voice, "Let your mom sleep. Come watch *Judge Judy* with me." Your thick brain, your heavy eyelids: *Get up and help him.* Then, unexpectedly: his agreement. Their footsteps down the hall.

Sneak into your parents' bedroom at midnight, after your son is finally asleep. Tell them, "I think we'll need to go to the hospital tomorrow. He's seeing things again." Tell them, "I thought the meds were working." When they offer to take the girls to school, say, "No, I've got it." Then stop. Say, "Actually, yes. Thank you." Say, "Thank you so much."

Come to uneasy terms with your husband's work travel. The money he makes from this job allowing you to stay home with your son. But the resentment. The way you've held on to it for so long. His confused look when you describe the smell of the emergency room, the cleaner they use that immediately triggers an adrenaline rush through your body. His nod when you tell him about the panic attack you had when you went to get a haircut yesterday, practically running from the crowded salon, realizing afterward that they used the same harsh cleaning solution and only your nose and heart recognized it. He tries to understand, but he can't. He's never smelled it. Forgive him, almost.

Lose your breath at your parents asking, “Can we take the kids out for ice cream?” How did they know your skin was crawling from too many fingers touching you? How could they tell that you were one meltdown away from your own? Your mask, has it cracked? Is it too worn? The pressure behind your eyes. Is it a migraine? Is it gratitude? “Yes, that’d be great.” The pressure eases a little, and your stomach growls. You haven’t eaten today. “Bring me back a root beer float?”

Have coffee with your husband in the kitchen, seven days in a row, after COVID shuts down everything. When your mother calls out, “Good morning!” from across the house, let your husband answer for the both of you. Let his contentment seep, just a little, into your body. The muscles in your neck and back relaxing as he refills your mug.

Watch your husband and your father build a family of snowmen with your children. Watch your son shove a carrot in the middle of each snow face. Watch him hold up his sister to place the raisin eyes. Watch his other sister complain about the eyes being crooked. Watch your father lecture everyone about cooperation. Watch your husband visibly practice patience with his father-in-law. Sip your coffee, still hot. Breathe in, breathe out.

Begin to work part-time for the first time in twelve years. Fall back in love with your husband. Thank your parents again, then again. Apply for graduate school. Get into graduate school. Are you crazy? You must be crazy. What selfish mother lets herself imagine such things? Who do you think you are?

Listen to your children’s loud complaints settle into whispers at the bedroom door. *Are you working, Mom? Are you writing your novel? Is Nana picking me up from school today? Is it okay if we get ice cream?*

You work. You write. You graduate. You change. You blink and you’ve spent five years in Virginia. You talk about the future with your husband, Google *remote teaching jobs*, Google *small New England beach towns.* Laugh until your stomach hurts, high on half a joint and an entire huge world of possibility. *The Eight Year Plan*, he calls it. By then your girls will be in college. By then, your son—who can know? "We have to try," your husband says. "We have to try," you answer.

Sit your parents down. Tell them about *the Eight Year Plan*. Your mother's eyes grow wide and sad, but she nods. You watch every thought play out across her face. The retirement home she never wanted to move into. The grandchildren she never thought would grow up. The family dinners, the vacations, the chaos she embraced with a grace you'd never seen from her before these years together. Realize this woman has grown into the caregiver you didn't have before. She's watched you every day, every hour. She's saved you and she knows it. She's saved you and it's changed her into the mother she always wanted to be.

Picture her shrinking body, sitting at your kitchen table and looking out at the sea. Picture her reaching up to adjust her hearing aid, listening for children's voices that no longer echo through the house. Picture her blowing on her tea, remembering, and your son, a man now, racing into the room to show both of you his quarter grades from the community college. Picture her delighted clap, his proud smile, the celebratory hamburgers you'll make, the evening drive to get soft serve.

"I'd like you to come with us."

PART II

INTENTIONAL COMMUNITIES

THE LIFE AND AFTERLIFE OF A SHARED HOME

Rhaina Cohen

We understood the math of mundane time together: the conversations in the kitchen as we scraped uneaten food off plates, leisurely walks to the playground on Saturdays—they'd add up to greater closeness.

Even before my husband and I moved in with two of our friends and their son, we knew this living arrangement would have an expiration date. We just didn't know how far ahead that date was.

I had casually brought up the idea of living together when the four adults caught up over Zoom in 2021. My husband and I sat at our dining table in Washington, DC, eating stew, as our friends Naomi and Daniel* ate their own meal hundreds of miles away. They told us they'd accepted jobs in DC and would move down from Boston in a few months. My passing comment about sharing a home was vapor that quickly condensed into a dream cloud. The four of us began imagining our future mini kibbutz, a communal settlement that comes from the Hebrew word *qibbūṣ*.

A question trailed our fantasy: Was creating a kibbutz worth the trouble? Naomi and Daniel didn't expect DC to be their long-term home. Naomi broke down the probabilities: 98 percent for two years, 90 for three years, 80 for four years, 20 for seven years. If we were going to live together for only a few years, buying a home didn't make

* To preserve the privacy of those mentioned in this essay, I use pseudonyms.

sense. The alternative—renting—felt like an unwise financial decision to me. My husband and I would have to leave our affordable rent-stabilized apartment for a more expensive shared space, which would slow our progress in saving for a down payment. But we decided we were willing to make this trade because of all the anticipated perks of life on the other side. Our shared home would be a hub for hosting; our friend circles would blend; our friends' one-year-old, Yonah, would be a housemate—a particular boon for my husband, who's known since childhood that he wants to have kids. (A friend recently described him as having "serious mom energy.") We understood the math of mundane time together: the conversations in the kitchen as we scraped uneaten food off plates, leisurely walks to the playground on Saturdays—they'd add up to greater closeness.

As leaves started to reemerge on barren winter branches, my husband and I visited homes in DC and reported back to our friends. When we toured a house with distinctive wood detailing and a pergola in the yard, I began daydreaming of the dinners we'd host outside, illuminated by string lights. We quickly put in an application and lost the bid. Then Naomi, who'd been obsessively tracking rental listings, saw a Craigslist post for a row house that ticked all our boxes for location, size, and sunlight. During the visit, I was taken with the gingko trees lining the street, the nine-foot ceilings, the crown molding in the living and dining rooms. But the place was unkempt. Long strips of dark green paint hung from the house's facade and metal bars on the windows blocked light. The landlord told us that the tenants were a rotating cast of recent college grads who left the house in such an unruly state that he started paying for a cleaner to come by regularly. We, by contrast, appeared to be responsible adults. When Naomi negotiated the rent price down by about 15 percent, I got an early lesson in her force of will.

We emailed the pdf of the lease back and forth until we had all four digital signatures. Never having lived together before—or even been on vacation together—we officially committed to being housemates.

We weren't naive or in denial about all that could go wrong. We set up a plan in case the living situation didn't work out: my husband and I would leave after a year, unless all the adults determined that we wanted to continue living together. And we did a "pre-mortem" instead of a postmortem, where you assess what went wrong after the fact. We assumed, as an exercise, that we didn't want to continue living together after a year and tried to identify the most likely reasons. I pictured being frustrated by the needs and noises of a young child. The three introverts thought it might be hard to unwind in a full house. We couldn't come up with a solution to every potential issue we identified. For instance, I hadn't spent much time around young kids, so I wasn't sure how I'd feel about a one-year-old's company. But we could try to prevent some, like establishing the norm that we didn't need to stop what we were doing to talk to a housemate who entered the same space. By addressing issues on the front end, maybe we'd avoid traps.

Our housing setup may have been temporary, but we didn't operate in a state of limbo. We quickly settled in. We asked the landlord to remove the bars from the windows and fix the protruding nails on the floorboards, and we split the cost to wax the wood floors. Within a week, Naomi had art framed and hung on the walls of our shared spaces. She created an organizational system for our kitchen, and even revised it. Her determination aside, we probably would have rushed to get the house in order because of Yonah by attaching childproof locks on the kitchen cabinets, installing baby gates on each staircase landing, anchoring bookshelves to the walls. Baby proofing has to happen immediately, whether you plan to live somewhere for one year or ten.

Shabbat dinner on Friday nights became our most meaningful housemate time. We established rituals: Naomi, Daniel, and I divvied up who said which blessing at dinner and sang the grace after the meal to my husband's preferred tune—"Chim Chim Cher-ee" from *Mary Poppins*. I instigated a conga line at the end of Shabbat, and we'd snake through the first floor while singing. When Yonah started learning to walk, my husband would take his hands and step backward as Yonah hobbled forward. A year and a half later, at the bris of our housemates' second child, my husband held the drowsy newborn as I announced his name—Jacob—to the dozens of family members and friends there to celebrate. Our commitment was temporary, but that didn't make it shallow.

Not long after, Naomi explained she was going on the academic job market, and I sensed we were at the beginning of the end. Professorships are few and far between, and if you're serious about getting a job, you must be willing to go just about anywhere in the country—the nerd equivalent of committing to life in the clergy or military. The odds that Naomi would end up at a school in the DC area were slim. If that wasn't hard enough, Daniel was vying for a position as a professor too. It's difficult for a couple to land academic jobs in the same place; there's even a term for it: the two-body problem.

My husband is typically hyper-logical, so I was thrown by his confidence that our friends would both find jobs nearby. We were back to talking about probabilities. I thought the chance that they'd stay was around 10 percent. He thought 70 to 80 percent. His belief felt to me like faith.

Within just a few months, Naomi and Daniel made a combined thirty or so trips to universities for interviews. On our kitchen shelf, branded thermoses they'd brought back from campus visits were like pins on a US map, marking schools across the country they'd visited—and all the places they could end up: Iowa, California, Missouri. Even as we learned that one DC-area school after another was out of the running, my husband remained optimistic that a local school would work out.

At last, Naomi and Daniel landed jobs at one of the top departments in the country for their field. It was an extraordinary feat, a vindication for the late hours spent researching and writing and sending endless thank you emails, all the while managing middle-of-the-night feedings for Jacob. They got lucky with geography:

their university was near family and close friends. But it was in New York. Solving the two-body problem proved far easier than the four-body one.

As their move approached, Naomi explained to three-year-old Yonah that Rhaina and Coco—Yonah's nickname for my husband—wouldn't move with them. He was distraught and kept asking, "Why?" "Why?" "Why?"

My husband and I didn't want our friends' departure to mark the end of our experience with communal living. Much like suburbanites get attached to quiet and leafy surroundings, we'd gotten used to the support and joys of sharing space with close friends. It was our new normal. We expected to have kids down the line and saw how much of a relief it was for other adults to simply be around, how it made parenthood less isolating. We wanted a living setup like we had with Naomi and Daniel, but one that could last far longer. A good friend of ours, Adam, shared this vision. And when he wanted something, he didn't just daydream about it. He acted on it.

Adam, my husband, and I planned a two-week trip to Oakland, California, treating it as a trial for living together. I noticed how swiftly Adam made decisions about where to get takeout—while I'd weigh the costs and benefits of eighteen options—and how calmly he shifted into problem-solving mode when we discovered his rental car had been towed. During the trip, the three of us spent hours on the porch discussing different possibilities for how we could intertwine our lives. We could have a three-parent family or, if Adam had a kid with a partner, raise our children as siblings.

Naomi and Daniel also looked ahead to another living arrangement built around friends. I was flattered that our home life had been rewarding enough that they wanted to replicate it. They strongly considered buying a house next to Naomi's best friend, but ultimately determined they couldn't afford it. Instead, they rented an apartment near family, friends, and a vibrant Jewish community. It wasn't exactly our model, but they could try to make it come close.

In our final weeks of living together, Naomi, Daniel, my husband, and I treated Shabbat dinners as events to savor, carefully selecting who to invite as guests. Our sentimentality coexisted with practicality. Naomi hired someone to remove the hardware in the walls and patch up the holes. I went through each kitchen cabinet, pulling out the items that belonged to my husband and me. After three years of sharing these supplies, I wasn't certain whose was whose. Were both bread loaf pans ours? What about the garlic press? Naomi noticed that the rubber spatula I'd taken was actually theirs. We were parting ways with mutual tenderness. How did couples manage this drudgery while splitting up? Each kitchen appliance a reminder that your hopeful experiment in merging your lives was over.

With the end in sight, I thought not just about the things I'd miss, but felt relief about changes ahead. When I tripped over a toy car in the living room, I pictured the oasis of an empty floor. Soon, I wouldn't have to pass a painting of the Angel of Death—an heirloom Naomi insisted on hanging even though she didn't particularly like it—every time I walked to or from my bedroom. A few times, I thought about mentioning the scattered toys or the painting, but I didn't want to complain when my friends were scrambling to care for their kids during one of the most intense periods in their professional lives. Bringing up things that bothered me was a muscle I wanted to strengthen as I lived with friends going forward.

We put a final house dinner on our joint Google calendar. It was the first time all of us had been to a restaurant together. We exchanged gifts and cards. Naomi trolled us by regifting a creepy talking teddy bear that she was eager to offload. I had hoped for some collective reflection, but with the kids interrupting conversation, that was hard to come by.

In the remaining hours at home, Naomi attached masking tape to furniture that belonged to my husband and me so that the movers knew what to leave in the house. My husband took the day of the move off from his job to spend time with Yonah. I ducked out of work for an hour and sat on the floor of my bedroom with the two of them. Yonah learned to line up an illustrated card deck, matching colors and putting the card numbers in order. Not as innately enchanted with children as my husband is, I hadn't spent all that much one-on-one time with Yonah and wondered if that was a mistake.

My husband and I rode the Metro with our friends to the train station, where they'd depart for their new city. Then I had to return to work. By the time I was home, my husband had changed the lock screen on his phone to a photo of him holding Jacob.

I've heard advice for long-distance couples that you shouldn't part ways without knowing the next time you'll see each other in person. My husband had already booked two round-trip train tickets to New York for each of the next two months. I had plans to stay with them about a week after their move.

I did a double take when I arrived at Naomi and Daniel's New York apartment. Daniel's parents, who joined us for Shabbat dinner, were sitting on the antique couch that used to be in Yonah's bedroom. Seeing the furniture and decor that used to be in my house in this new space—one that wasn't my own—felt off, like a familiar song transposed into a different key.

But it wasn't just that the same items from our three-floor home were redistributed into a one-floor apartment. There was a stately display cabinet in the entryway that I hadn't seen before and other furniture that Naomi and Daniel had recently bought. And there was a new person: a nineteen-year-old au pair, who had arrived just days ago from a small town in Israel. Living with us made Naomi and Daniel more open to inviting a teenager from another country to stay with them. The risk calculus felt similar: high potential upside, low downside if it goes wrong.

I tried to help in the kitchen but quickly realized that I didn't know where things were. Did they have a water filter? Where were the table linens? I didn't want to aimlessly open cabinets; it would feel intrusive and only underscore that this was not my home, these were not my things. The au pair was more familiar with the kitchen than I was.

A month later, my husband and I stayed with our friends together, although he took an earlier train than I did. When he walked in the apartment door, the first thing Yonah said was, "Where's Rhaina?" I had worried that the kids might be less comfortable around us now that we weren't seeing them as much. But when I got there, I squatted down and asked Yonah if I could have a hug. He walked into my arms. Jacob, just over a year old, took a bit longer to look at me with familiar eyes. At this point, I had been absent for one-twelfth of his life.

It became clear to me that my husband and I would inevitably lose some of the closeness we shared with the kids. We didn't have opportunities to hear what new bird species Yonah was learning to identify or how he managed his jealousy as a big brother. We didn't see how Jacob had progressed from halting steps to confident waddling. When I watched him run across the living room in a video Daniel sent to our group chat, I realized I had missed another milestone. As the boys got older, I wondered, who would we be to them? Both Yonah and Jacob were young enough that they probably wouldn't remember all the time we spent in the same home.

But that didn't mean we were starting from scratch. The meals we ate, the songs we sang, the conga lines we danced in the house—they'd formed a rope for my husband and me to hang on to, tying us to the kids. As long as we didn't let go, we remained tethered to them.

A couple months after Naomi and Daniel moved, my husband asked to call Yonah that evening for his fourth birthday, but he forgot to call before Yonah's bedtime. That night, Naomi sent us a video of Yonah talking to the screen, asking, "Where's Coco?" My husband started watching the video but couldn't make it through the whole three minutes. He felt too guilty. We watched it together in bed. In the video, Naomi fielded Yonah's questions about Coco's absence. Yonah talked about art he made that he wanted to give me. He asked his mom when my husband and I were moving to New York because it was the best.

The summer after my husband, our friend Adam, and I had our trial run in Oakland, my husband and I returned to the Bay Area for vacation. By then, Adam had moved his things into our house. He agreed to live with us for six months to start; he'd recently quit his job and was recovering from a breakup. At that exact moment, he didn't feel ready for a long-term commitment.

During a barbecue at a friend's house in San Francisco, an acquaintance and I commiserated about a situation we'd each witnessed in our respective cities. A friend had told her that he didn't know how long he'd be in San Francisco, so it didn't feel worth it to try to build close ties. His caution was understandable—except it's now been five years, and he's still in San Francisco.

On that same trip, I went on a group hike that included a close friend, Rachel, who had recently accepted a temporary job in DC, and her partner. My husband, Adam, and I eventually offered Rachel a spot in our house. Although she and Adam had never met in person, I had a hunch that we would all mesh well. By the time Rachel had moved in, she was no longer in a relationship with the partner on that hike. I thought of the unwitting San Francisco resident. The things we expect to be temporary can last. And the things we expect to last can be temporary.

We don't have any children living in our house now, yet it feels childlike. Once we realized that the first initials of our names spell "ARRR," pirate jokes ensued. I dubbed us "housemateys." The four of us filled out a chart with a few habits that we're trying to develop—doing physical therapy exercises or calling our parents each week—and one day, I noticed a new habit had been added to each person's list: "Bury treasure." "Polish hook." The living room quickly became a place for impromptu dancing and jamming, with more instruments than there are housemates. The night Rachel moved in, with her legs swung over the side of an armchair as we talked, I thought, *I've hacked adulthood.* We had signed up for a continuous sleepover.

But enjoying this new configuration so much felt almost like a betrayal. If this incarnation of the house was so great, I feared my enthusiasm about the last setup was less genuine. My zero-sum mentality eased when I'd notice the lasting imprint of our kibbutz. I could chant the Shabbat prayers by heart because I had recited them again and again alongside my friends. When a friend's kid would ask me questions that seemed too complicated to answer, I'd remember how Daniel effortlessly gave sophisticated but understandable answers to Yonah's questions. (The last time I visited, Yonah asked why we had lived together if the four grown-ups weren't all married to each other. Daniel then asked Yonah if the two of them were married. Yonah said, "No!," eyes wide at the absurdity of the idea. Daniel replied, "See, you don't need to be married to live together.") A shared home—whether with one partner, family members, or friends—shapes everyone who lives within its walls. My time with Naomi, Daniel, and their kids didn't just lay the groundwork for an ongoing relationship with them and their children. It was a chapter that changed who I would be in the future chapters of my life.

About a week into our new living situation, Adam, Rachel, my husband, and I had dinner at another friend's house. We went around the table telling stories about the weirdest experiences we've ever had. Rachel explained her love of April Fools' Day and an ill-conceived but impressively elaborate prank she pulled the prior year. Adam looked at my husband and me, his eyes alert with playful warning. "Watch out," he said. I thought to myself, *April 1 is half a year away; Rachel will probably have already moved out by then.* But as my new housemates regaled the other guests with their humor and wonky obsessions, I thought, being surrounded by these friends every day is going to make me smarter, more compassionate, and sillier, no matter how long our living arrangement lasts.

Q&A *with* SUANNE CARLSON

I don't consider myself homeless. I'm at home in nature, and I consider my vehicle shelter. I get so much from living this way: the freedom, the nature, the community of like-minded people, the very small carbon footprint compared to what it used to be.

When Homes on Wheels Alliance (HOWA) president Bob Wells asked Suanne Carlson to become the emerging organization's first executive director, Suanne had been living on the road full-time for less than a year, but Bob knew she was the right person for the job. A trusted, detail-oriented friend with a background in higher education policy, Suanne had the experience and approach to complement Bob's vision to serve nomads in need. Her three stipulations for accepting the job? That she would continue to live on the road, that she would become a cofounder of the organization, and that she would do the work without financial compensation.

In less than a decade, Bob and Suanne have implemented programs offering financial support, vehicles, education, resources, and training to thousands of nomads—people who live and travel in their vehicles by choice or because of life circumstances. They've also prioritized community, organizing caravans—two-week campouts allowing nomads to meet up with one another—and extending outreach and curriculum for their annual Rubber Tramp Rendezvous (RTR), the largest gathering of nomads in the world.[1]

In 2018, Suanne established the Women's Rubber Tramp Rendezvous (WRTR), an annual gathering focused on empowering women nomads and providing information about safety and hygiene on the road.[2] Suanne, now in her seventies, recently retired from her executive director role, but she serves on HOWA's board of trustees as vice president and is an active leader within the organization. Based in Nevada, she takes her hybrid off-road SUV to temperate climates such as Arizona, Florida, and South Texas in the winter, and travels to see friends and family in Oregon, California, and Washington in the summer.

People have become more familiar with the nomad lifestyle since the release of Jessica Bruder's book *Nomadland* and the Academy Award–winning film adaptation in which Bob and Suanne appeared. In our conversation, Suanne shared additional insight into embracing the freedom of a life on the road and the support of a community of like-minded individuals.

What inspired you to start camping part-time in 2009? What led you to live on the road full-time in 2016?

When I was fifty-three, my daughter was diagnosed with a cancerous brain tumor. She was twenty-nine and had a four-year-old child. One of the main things that came out of a year's worth of therapy after she passed was that I still had lots more grief work to do, and going on the road was how I needed to do it. Why I knew that, I don't know. I had never done road trips or lived out of my vehicle before. I did have a small teardrop trailer that I loved camping out of every once in a while, so I knew I liked living small. I used to drive to work in a Prius, and it just occurred to me one day that I could set up the Prius like our teardrop, and I could use that as my road trip vehicle.

Over about six months, my goal was to be in nature as much as possible. That's when I discovered the van dwelling community, which they were called at that time. I found that I could learn a lot about how they lived in their vehicles for my road trip. In the spring of 2010, I set off solo to visit the national parks from coast to coast. Going on the road was akin to letting go—praying, getting angry, grieving. Then when I landed at a national park, it was akin to filling up, being healed. It's not an unusual story for people on the road that this is a way for them to deal with loss, whether loss of a spouse, loss of a child, loss of the ability to work, loss of health, or financial loss.

Between 2010 and 2016, I would be on the road for months at a time. Because I realized that I really needed to travel and be in nature consistently, and my husband didn't want to be away from home, we grew apart. We amicably divorced at the end of 2016, and that is when I went on the road full-time.

Did you face stigma from relatives or friends at first—or even still—for this choice? How about from society at large?

Society at large, and the federal government in particular, considers me homeless. I don't consider myself homeless. I'm at home in nature, and I consider my vehicle shelter. Because of federal regulations and societal norms, I have a physical address that I can call home that's required for me to even get a driver's license or insurance. I rent a room, and it's a shame that I have to pay the cost because I'm not there, but thankfully, it's with a good friend. He gets a little income, and I get to use his address as my official place of residence and have a little storage. I went into this lifestyle knowing that there was this stigma, and it's worth it to me. I get so much from living this way: the freedom, the communion with nature, the community of like-minded people, the very small carbon footprint compared to what it used to be.

But the rock rolls downhill to how society and, more specifically, family look at me. When I would sometimes spend Thanksgivings at my cousins' houses, they wanted me to come inside for the night instead of sleeping in my Prius. This came from a place of love, but their thinking was, "Well, of course, you'd want to do that because you sleep in your car. That's just terrible." And finally, I said to them, "Imagine if you could bring your bedroom with you. Would you rather sleep in your bedroom or in somebody else's house?" And the light bulb went on. They realized this was my home that was parked at their curb. It wasn't just a vehicle that I was temporarily living in and it wasn't less than their bedroom in their house. That kind of acceptance happened over a couple of years.

It's interesting that there are people who, even when they're presented with this lifestyle, still see it as a bad choice, like a choice that nobody should ever make. I followed the movie *Nomadland* quite closely and watched the public's reaction. Some people really got the movie and saw this as a viable choice for the main character and other people thought it was dark and sad and terrible. It was really telling for me.

Was loneliness something you were worried about when you considered becoming a nomad?

I lived in my little town in Washington state for twenty-five years. I knew my neighbors and I would say we were neighbors, not friends. I had colleagues at work who I liked, but other than my husband, I didn't really have anybody I felt close to. Then I went on that first trip to the national parks and met up with a small group that included Bob Wells and some other folks. They made a conscious choice that this is how and where they were going to live, and that like-mindedness created a sense of connection that I had not fully felt before. So I wasn't really worried about loneliness, but I think most women, especially older women, are afraid of being lonely. The caravans that HOWA organizes provide a way for them to step out on their own toward community, and they find connections there.

Not only do nomads experience this kind of instant connection, having committed to these unique values surrounding how we live, but when we get together, because we are transient, we don't waste time with surface discussions. We get to the meat of who we are—not politics or religion—but we talk about things that are important to us. One of the norms that I've tried to instill is that we focus on what we have in common because we have so much more in common than not. Let's avoid those topics that are divisive and focus on those things that bring us together, like why we chose to live this way in the first place, and on helping each other. I think we need to embrace as individuals that it's more important to be kind than it is to be right.

What have you learned about communal living and creating community through caravaning?

What's pretty unique here is that I can be an integral part of a community and I can still be alone when I need to. People learn when they're around after a while not to be offended when somebody just gets up and leaves, because there are a lot of introverts here. There are also a significant number of individuals with PTSD who can get triggered, and they just need to leave. In this community, it's the norm not to take that personally. It's really a learned reaction—at least it was for me. I think some people equate it to having the freedom to do whatever you want in terms of staying or going, and it's not a measure of how much they like you. It's just a sense of freedom to address whatever their needs are in that moment without the social graces. It's the same thing with parking hundreds of yards apart. When you think about camping with a group, you might imagine a campground where people are feet apart. With caravans, people could be a quarter mile away and still be part of the group.

Has joining the nomad community led you to understand yourself and the world around you in new and different ways?

HOWA is 60 to 65 percent women, primarily older women. I would say the mean age is sixty-five. And their stories are often: I did what society said. I stayed and was the mother. I might have gone out and worked, but my primary focus was home and family. I gave my all, and my husband has either died or left, and I don't have money to live in a house anymore, or I haven't ever followed my dreams, and so now this is my time. In my generation, and I'm sure others too, woman were socialized to take care of everybody. To have the norms of the community be that it's a good thing to take care of yourself, whatever that means—camping by yourself for this season, or camping with people for that season—is a really powerful message for women my age.

I know for you, being a nomad is a choice rather than something you had to do for economic reasons. Can you tell me about the work HOWA has done to support nomads who are more economically at risk?

Some people, and Bob is a good example, have to move into a vehicle because they cannot afford a conventional living situation. Bob's vision for HOWA was to help those who were economically in crisis by providing vehicles for them to live out of, as well as helping those who had vehicles to make them functional as homes. Labor coordination is done by paid staff, but all vehicle home-builds, solar installations, shelving, insulation, and ventilation is done by volunteers within the nomadic community. It became extremely obvious as we were continuing with our mission to help those in financial need that we had to have this community component for these folks to be successful and, along with adopting the caravans and the RTR, this led HOWA's mission to evolve to include community building. Even during a recent period where HOWA's volunteers couldn't help make vehicles functional as homes due to liability insurance constraints, I saw the community step up and provide that on a person-to-person level, outside of HOWA. This took the form of Facebook posts where somebody would say, "I'm going to be at the next RTR so if anybody needs help with their electrical, let me know," and they gave their credentials. That was great to watch.

Another way we help people who are struggling financially is by having an emergency fund. If people are in need, if their personal emergency fund is gone and their transmission fails, they can apply for cash assistance through HOWA. Since the beginning of this year, we've granted about $23,000 to help nomads in that kind of situation.[3]

What kinds of changes in the ways society thinks about nomads and community would you like to see?

I'd like them to see this as a valid, dignified choice for a person. The stigma is so ingrained in our policies, our laws, and our culture. For example, people camping in the national forest, especially in Arizona, will be cited for camping if they seem not to have a home. If you're vacationing, it's fine, but if you're not, then you're illegally camping. The leadership of public lands, like us, can see that there's a housing crisis, that people are more and more going to not be able to afford to live in conventional housing. If that's the case, where are they going to live? And I believe these public managers are being proactive and saying not on public land because we are charged with protecting it. I can articulate and understand their argument, but I don't agree with it. I think there's compromises to be had. One of the things that I practice and that HOWA teaches, for example, is good land stewardship. When you leave a place, it shouldn't look like you've been there. And not only that, if there was trash there when you pulled up, you take that trash.

For me, nature feels like an entity, like a companion, in a way that I miss it when I'm in town or with family at their homes. The word *community*, or *communing*, is key. Living in nature feels very much aligned with communal living. And a healthy community—a healthy society—has to be inclusive of lifestyles, which includes the lifestyle of what you choose to call home.

THE ART OF AGING IN COMMUNITY

Kate Madden Yee

> *We're not all best friends here, but inherent in the cohousing model is an overall desire to seek the health of the group.*

The face of my eighty-five-year-old neighbor Louise is a map of life experience. Her keen blue eyes have witnessed decades of social change, from early civil and women's rights movements to the assassinations of President John F. Kennedy and Martin Luther King Jr. to the Cuban missile crisis and Vietnam War. She cradles her tea mug and smiles encouragingly as we sit at the snug table in her rented studio home, her high cheekbones framed by two silver gray braids that hang down to her shoulders. Born and raised in California, in Berkeley and Napa, Louise has spent her life as a writer, teacher, Buddhist practitioner, and social activist—devoting herself to peace initiatives, racial justice, antinuclear efforts, and caring for the earth. For fifteen years we've been neighbors in the Oakland, California, cohousing community I cofounded, and I value her as a powerful example of aging gracefully.

My husband, Randy, and I joined our cohousing community when I was twenty-eight. We met during our undergraduate years at UC Santa Cruz in a Christian fellowship where we learned to prioritize community over the nuclear family–oriented American Dream of suburban life. When we arrived in Oakland in 1997, we were already veterans of shared housing. Both of us had lived with roommates and together had rented an apartment with a young family during my graduate studies. At our new church, we connected with a team of couples and singles interested in using the cohousing model as a way to be of service in a specific Oakland neighborhood. We wanted to put down roots in an urban setting, tutor at the local school, and "live lightly on the earth" by installing solar panels to generate energy and sharing resources such as cars, tools, and laundry machines. When Randy and I decided to participate, I wasn't thinking of what growing old in cohousing might look like. Instead, I was enamored with what felt like an avant-garde faith practice of creating community literally from the ground up.

Cohousing is an intentional neighborhood fostered by people who seek to live with others who share their values. Most cohousing in the United States is made up of specially designed condominium developments where members buy their homes at market rate and pay their own mortgages. Of course, this can be expensive and impractical depending on the circumstances, so in urban areas where land is scarce, some cohousers find and buy adjacent homes in a model called retrofit cohousing. Every kind of cohousing complex is centered around shared spaces, including a common house. Ours contains a kitchen, a dining and laundry area, a bathroom, and a living room. We also tend a vegetable garden and share a tool shed, bicycle storage, and a small gym we've created in the barn.

In 1998, our group bought an empty lot in North Oakland and acted as our own developers, hiring a cohousing architect and a contractor, interacting with the city regarding necessary zoning changes, and putting in months of sweat equity by demolishing creaky garages and scraping old lead paint off the existing house and barn. The project kept me both exhilarated and exhausted, but my deeply held drive to commitment—especially when it came to faith community—undergirded it all. Although none of my fellow cohousers explicitly said, "Sign here indicating you will never leave," that was the rubric under which I was operating. I was all in.

Our community consists of nine households. We initially had thirty residents, nine of whom were children. The first generation of kids, including my two sons, has grown up and moved away, but we have a new cohort of youngsters, who range in age from four to ten.

Our life together revolves around spontaneous meetups on the back lawn for a cold beverage or a round of croquet, weekly meals we take turns cooking in the common kitchen and share in our common dining room, and monthly "work parties" to care for our property. Having a built-in community is often as natural and joyful as I initially hoped it would be.

Still, when you're twenty-eight, it's hard to imagine thirty, let alone fifty-five. So much has changed in over twenty years of cohousing, and while there's been lots of goodness, there have also been moments of disillusionment and frustration. My relationship to the faith that originally drew me to this way of life has shifted, and the daily reality of communal living has sometimes left me longing for a different path. We've had thorny monthly owners' meetings where we try to reach consensus about how much of our yard should be food-growing garden space, revise the bylaws that govern our community practices, or develop guidelines about renovations in individual homes. I've experienced conflicts around parenting and communication styles, the challenge of relating to a range of people with different personalities and temperaments in close quarters, and the physical exhaustion of the monthly work days as I get older. I have also struggled with the painful realities of city life in Oakland—homelessness, civil unrest, racism, poverty—and how to most effectively engage with city leadership and local activists around these issues, which some of my neighbors and I have tried to do through participating in protests, contributing supplies for immigrant students at the nearby international high school, and attending Oakland city council meetings.

Yet I can't deny that these challenges coexist with deeply satisfying, soul-nourishing moments of connection with my fellow cohousers. Those moments of connection have only grown deeper and more frequent with age and time. I've become a closer listener as I eat lunch with a neighbor at the picnic table under our magnolia tree and hear about the difficulties of raising a young child with special needs. That same neighbor joins me as the community comes together over the backyard firepit to mark with meditation and prayer the untimely passing of another member's sibling. Even an activity as simple as spontaneously making chalk drawings in the courtyard with one of the children is something I might not have access to anymore if not for cohousing. And because of those monthly owners' meetings, I've gotten better at communicating my needs and thoughts more clearly.

Lately, I've started to consider how I might shape the landscape of my remaining years. When it comes to aging with purpose and integrity, and determining if growing old in cohousing is the right path, I look to my neighbor Louise.

Louise entered into this cohousing experiment nearly fifteen years ago, when she was in her early seventies. Her addition to our community expanded its generational range. Today, we have representation of almost every decade. Our youngest member is four and Louise is our oldest. She has brought deep experience and wisdom to our community life, sharing expert gardening skills, peace and meditation practices, and healthy food for our common meals.

After earning a PhD in English literature at UC Berkeley in the 1960s, Louise spent more than forty years in Boston, where she taught at MIT. In the midst of the Vietnam War, she and her peers questioned the traditional narrative of American life, and part of this included exploring the idea of shared housing, although she didn't pursue it until she bought a stake in a Cambridgeport twelve-unit limited-equity co-op in 1994. When she moved back to California in 2009, she found our cohousing group through one of our former members, who also happened to be the publisher of her first book, and rented one of the available studios.

Joining cohousing in California was both a fulfillment of Louise's desire to continue living in community and a dramatic change after decades on the East Coast. When she first moved in, she'd wake up feeling a rush of joy being back in the place where she grew up. She was still in good health, mountain climbing, taking care of family land in Napa, organizing and participating in peace walks, and engaging with her Buddhist sangha. But as the years went by, Louise began to notice that her active lifestyle was catching up with her. She experienced a handful of significant health concerns, including a house dust allergy that briefly forced her out of her apartment, a concussion, an ovarian cyst, and a heart attack. She felt our community's support during these crises, particularly with the heart attack, as her cohousing neighbors helped her get to the emergency room, visited her in the hospital, and checked in regularly once she was back home.

When Louise chose to live in cohousing in her seventies, she didn't anticipate the level of physical support she might eventually need since she was in such good shape. But having a close, intentional community became vital as she learned how to shift the way she took care of herself by asking for assistance from family, friends, and neighbors. Although aging and illness were changing Louise's sense of self and independence, she continued her commitment to social justice. At the age of eighty-four, she published a book that explored her family's settler legacy in Napa, noting how it has been part of the theft of Indigenous land. I admire Louise both for her dedication to social justice and her flexibility in adapting to the demands of aging.

I've given a lot of thought to whether cohousing could provide me and my similarly aged neighbors with the right support moving through the last third of our lives, as it has for Louise. There's certainly potential for helping each other navigate increasing physical limitations. Over the years, we've supported other cohousing members through mental illness, stroke, and cancer by providing additional meals, rides to medical appointments, and help with picking up prescriptions and groceries. In the future, if the work of making community meals becomes too labor-intensive, we might be able to share the cost of hiring a cook. We could use a similar strategy for maintaining individual homes and the community yard. House swapping might be another benefit of cohousing—and perhaps less stressful than the typical downsizing process many aging people face. Maybe a younger family could buy our four-bedroom home, and Randy and I could move into their two-bedroom unit. Somehow that feels more manageable when so much about aging feels overwhelming.

The deeper advantages of aging in cohousing may be less logistical and more relational. There's our shared history and values, and the joy of interacting daily with a wide variety of generations. On top of that, I'd have the support of neighbors willing to act as sounding boards as I think through retirement from my career as a medical journalist, evolving relationships with adult children—and perhaps future grandchildren—and the inevitable losses that come with aging, such as the deaths of parents and siblings.

Louise says about interdependent cohousing relationships: "You don't have to love everybody, but you can still have a connection to them." We're not all best friends here, but inherent in the cohousing model is an overall desire to seek the health of the group. Although my neighbors and I are different in our temperaments, energy, emotional capacities, and spiritual practices, we've worked hard to set up a community that is flexible and compassionate enough to hold each of us as we age. Perhaps that's the most important benefit of aging in cohousing: witnessing the life stages we all go through. More than once I've invited my neighbors to participate in rituals to mark particular age-related transitions. When I was thirty-two and my youngest son stopped nursing, I asked the women in my community to come over to discuss the grief I was feeling as I moved out of this stage of motherhood. When I turned forty, I threw a party that included 1980s dance tunes and a bouncy house in our common backyard. And when I turned fifty, my neighbors honored me with affirming cards and letters that boosted my morale as I ventured further into middle age. While these celebrations may not be unique to cohousing, I have found it profoundly meaningful to mark important milestones alongside people with whom I have shared decades of common life.

Randy and I are still in conversation about our future plans. Moving out of Oakland, and cohousing, is a possibility. But with elderly parents nearby and our children still needing a home base, we don't foresee a move anytime soon. On the practical side, our home doesn't require navigating stairs to get into and we're close to transit, medical care, and good restaurants. But most importantly, when I think of what I originally sought out of cohousing—a sense of community, resource sharing, and the ability to be of service—I'm not so sure I want to give that up.

RETURNING TO OSPAYE

Rodney M. Bordeaux

In order for us to get back to that pride and strength in ourselves and as a people, we need to restore our communities based upon our culture, and the family and community structures that support it.

Long before the Europeans and others came upon our shores of North America, Native Nations were a thriving people, some with permanent communities. Others were nomadic and moved around as the food supply, climate, and water resources dictated. We were not savages. We were not lost or needing to be civilized. We already had existing and healthy communities from our perspective. Our language and culture were extraordinarily strong before our first contact with Europeans and others. In order for us to get back to that pride and strength in ourselves and as a people, we need to restore our communities based upon our culture, and the family and community structures that support it.

My tribal nation, the Sicangu Lakota—or the Rosebud Sioux Tribe, as we are known to the federal, state, and local governments—inhabited the northern Great Plains of the United States. On these lands, our people lived and our government operated within a family structure that extended to a bigger community unit. This is composed of the *tiwahe* (family), *tiospaye* (extended families), *wicoti* (village), *ospaye* (community), and *oyate* (entire tribe or nation).

The tiwahe consists of the *ateh*, or father, and *ina/ena*, or mother. As caretaker of the home, the ina manages every aspect of language, customs, and culture, and she consults with the ateh on all matters concerning child-rearing and basic family needs. The ateh oversees the organization of the family, gathering and moving the tiwahe from one location to the next, roaming with the game and seasons. The tiospaye includes other branches of the family tree, such as children, grandparents, and cousins. Before the late 1800s, it was common to have up to ten lodges that form the tiospaye unit. Each lodge could have a warrior, selected by the tiospaye, to represent them outside of the home, especially with hunting.[1] Multiple tiospayes make up small villages of relatives, or wicoti. The next level of government, ospaye, contains four or more tiospayes and can have up to eight hundred members. Finally, the oyate encompass all the previous levels mentioned. My tribal nation is an oyate, and each of the 550-plus federally recognized tribes in the United States is considered an oyate. The whole family and nation are more unified with these defined roles and structural support.

Native Nations all enjoyed our own ways of life, through our native language and culture. With the federal policy of colonization, the objective was to destroy our culture and language and to force us to assimilate. As our families were torn apart through the mandatory participation in the federal boarding school policy of the late 1870s, these family, community, and government systems were not allowed to function properly. The goal of the federal boarding school policy was to "kill the Indian and save the man," destroying all Indian cultures in the United States. The breakup of our culture and language had an adverse effect on our family and traditional government structure. These elements couldn't be shared as the tiospayes were disbanded and had to move away from each other. Such was the end of our nomadic lifestyle and communities based on our cultural and family systems.

After we were confined to reservations, our people moved up to four times to find a suitable home. Rosebud, South Dakota, where I live now with my wife, son, and two grandchildren, was founded in the 1880s.[2] It was chosen for a permanent home, or tribal headquarters, by Chief Spotted Tail. Twenty communities were formed on our reservation with no opportunity for the tiospaye to function as a wicoti and ospaye because parents were not able to raise their own kids and instill our values in them, under the federal boarding school policy. As a result, the oyate structure fell apart and became disorganized.

The settlement acts of the early 1900s also took most of our best farmland. Our reservation lands—approximately 3.3 million acres in 1889—have been reduced to 950,178 acres, where our communities are scattered today.[3] As relatives no longer lived in one community, generations couldn't identify where they came from, what they represented, or how they were supported. This loss of identity and pride in family and village, combined with economic struggle, had a detrimental effect on individual and communal well-being, leading to violence, abuse of drugs and alcohol, and mental health challenges.

This was the cultural landscape I was born into in 1952. Our population was a mixture of Sicangu Lakota and whites. The government employees, Lakota and white, lived in government-owned single-family homes, with electricity, water, and sewer. The rest of the Sicangu Lakota lived in small log homes, two-room houses, shacks, and used trailers. Some families even lived in tents year-round. This substandard housing was segregated from the government housing. Most of the Lakota housing lacked electricity, water, and sewer, and due to high unemployment rates and scarcity of other resources, like public housing and credit, alternatives were few. My father worked for the Bureau of Indian Affairs (BIA), so we were fortunate to live in government quarters. I remember our relatives coming to bathe and listen to radios. In my first or second grade, however, my father lost his job with the BIA, so we had to vacate our home and move in with my aunt and her four sons in a two-bedroom house. The overcrowding led to tense situations between my mother and her sister. My dad, like many others, was forced to sell his 160 acres of land for pennies on the dollar in order to buy our family a used trailer house.

Although it was a drastic change, these circumstances were a way of life for so many people, and we made the best of it.

The US Department of Housing and Urban Development (HUD) was created in 1965, and tribes began to form housing authorities. Our first housing development began with four-cluster developments in the four largest of our twenty communities. It was the first time that most of our people had experienced living with water and sewer systems as well as other utilities and roads. Even though they look fine, HUD houses are one-size-fits-all. The same design is used in all parts of the country—from Alaska to the desert Southwest—without consideration for individual tribes in various geographies and climates, and with different cultural needs.

The HUD program was far from enough. Tribal housing continues to be underfunded and overcrowded, and a housing crisis persists on most Native American land.

My own path took me away from the reservation in search of better options. Through a government relocation program, I attended welding school in San Jose, California, where I worked as a certified welder for a few months. There, I was exposed to the Native American rights movement. I decided to return home and go to college with the hope of working for my tribe. I was determined to develop our government and serve my people—and I did, spending twelve years on our tribal council and ten years as president.

Part of my mission has been to restore the many losses we have incurred due to colonization and genocide. Even in my own family, the tiospaye is more distant than I would like it to be. But the Sicangu Lakota people are currently working on language and cultural restoration. We are fortunate to have members who have resisted colonization efforts and have kept these elements alive. These members, particularly those that speak the Lakota language, are deeply knowledgeable about our culture. They know the old ways of governance, community, and daily life. This information is passed down in stories and conversations with like-minded individuals and families. It begins with the tiospaye and expands through the wicoti. These families are more likely to share common values and see the need for communities. They also want to invest in our reservation through small business development so we can bring money back to our ospaye instead of spending eighty to ninety cents on the dollar in other communities.

I have heard of and witnessed families starting to establish the necessary resources to construct nonconventional, non-HUD homes. On our neighboring reservation, the Oglala Lakota are building dome-shaped homes that are energy efficient and affordable. In most of Indian country, all over the United States, I've noticed the development of housing that isn't funded by HUD, with more traditional designs from our respective cultures. This will occur more and more as tribes become financially stable, unburdened by government regulations. There is a rejuvenation happening.

I have also seen communities or large tiospayes where the Lakota language is alive and being actively taught to the children and others. These close communities have gatherings for all their people, share food and prayer, and teach language to people of all ages. This unity is key to development in all areas of life.

If we as Sicangu Lakota want to return to the traditional model of government, we must first ensure that our tiwahe structure is stable, which means basic needs like housing, food, and safety are met, and that there are clear roles for parents who provide, elders who guide, and children who participate. Families are also strengthened through cultural grounding—learning and speaking the Lakota language, practicing traditions, and honoring responsibilities across generations. This would naturally lay the foundation for smaller family units to be more intentional around larger tiospayes, as they reestablish connections among extended families, move from individual choices back toward collective deliberation with respected elders as the ultimate leaders, and share responsibilities by pooling resources for child-rearing and community obligations. With these solid foundations, we can then build our wicotis and ospayes into effective units. This will result in a more powerful oyate. While our people understand these concepts, we need to guide them in how to fully live by them. This instructional effort should be organized, beginning with the tiwahes and incorporating into our school curriculums. It will take a tremendous educational process for our people to be able to govern themselves again.

We are the ones responsible for instilling pride in our people and developing communities based upon our language and cultural values. Establishing stronger communities around our traditional family structure is key. I see myself as one person dedicated to serving my people so that we can all be a part of the effort to rebuild our nation. We choose to remain who we are, Lakota, and it is up to each one of us to get there. We must continue to lay the seed for the next generation to progress down this path.

Q&A *with* TIFFANY HARRIS

We're always looking for a big viral moment or a rally to move the needle, but what really moves the needle are these deep interpersonal relationships that you work through when spending time with or living alongside others.

As a child, Tiffany Harris spent a lot of time reading alone in her room while her mom was at work. She felt lonely without more people around, and she noticed the way her mom struggled without the support of nearby friends and family. Inside the apartment she shared with her mom and older brother, Tiffany sought out stories about characters who were mixed-race like her, surrounded by the larger families and broader communities that she dreamed of one day having.

"I had to imagine this world that I wanted to be in," she says.

Tiffany, now in her late thirties, has become a convener of community. Her first foray into communal living was when she stayed with host families in Morocco as a Peace Corps volunteer. After that, she attended graduate school in political science at Tel Aviv University, and seeking Jewish community upon her return to the United States, she moved into one of Washington, DC's Moishe Houses, a network of more than one hundred residential communities around the world for Jewish young adults. For nearly three years, Tiffany cohosted almost two hundred events with over five thousand attendees in the home she shared with her roommates. In 2020, she became chief program officer of Mem Global, the organization that runs the Moishe House initiative. She leads teams helping current residents host dinners related to Jewish culture and organize social events and Jewish education programs. Tiffany and I discussed her personal and professional experiences with co-living, belonging, and identity, as well as her predictions for the future of communal living in the US.

What did you learn about communal living while in the Peace Corps in Morocco?

My host families treated me like a Moroccan young woman. I had to be home before dark, I had to dress a certain way, I couldn't cook my own food. But even though I didn't have the degree of freedom or privacy that I wanted with my host families, there was something so beautiful about witnessing the intergenerational living that's common in Morocco. With my upbringing, I wasn't used to as much activity in the house, but there was something very special and healthy about it. I never felt alone or lonely. And I saw how from the time a baby is born until they grow old, they have this built-in network and family structure, often including grandparents. When you live communally, you give up something, whether that's privacy or a degree of space or anonymity, but you gain so much more by being surrounded by people and feeling held by the community.

How did you learn about Moishe House, and what led you to want to explore co-living?

When I returned to the States after the Peace Corps and going to grad school in Israel, I hadn't been home in almost six years. It was a shock, coming back from a place that's centered around the Jewish calendar, which allowed me to be more passive in my observance. But Judaism was something that really fulfilled me and I realized that I was going to have to be a lot more intentional about it in the States. I started looking for Jewish opportunities and someone told me about Moishe House. I applied to live there in 2014, and I lived with four or five roommates for two and a half years.

I absolutely loved living in a Moishe House, and I wish I could have done it for longer. It was fun being the front door of a community and getting to say to people, "If you enjoy these events, keep coming back. We're always happy to host you. Bring your friends." But I took on a global role in my job at the time where I'd be overseas for a month, and because I respected and genuinely loved my roommates, I didn't think it was fair to them that I wasn't going to be around to give 110 percent to planning and hosting events. After Moishe House, I even moved into another group house! I wasn't ready to live alone and I didn't stop having roommates until very recently.

Did co-living feel different from the typical roommate arrangement?

Co-living in a Moishe House is definitely different, and if you're living intentionally in any situation where you have a shared mission of some kind, I imagine it's distinct from typical roommates in a similar way. You're roommates, but you're also working together on something that takes up a lot of time—and you have to want to hang out with each other in addition to being able to work together. You need to be really in sync and responsible to each other in a way that you don't necessarily have to be in other roommate situations. Living in a Moishe House, if I say I'm going to be home at 4 p.m. to help set up a monthly Shabbat dinner or a social event, I need to be there out of respect for the community that I'm serving but also out of respect for my roommates.

What were the benefits of living in a communal environment through Moishe House? What were the drawbacks?

It was very cost effective, especially for the first couple of years I was in DC. I had tons of student loans and I was able to pay them off because of communal living. I also built resiliency. It was always in my mind that because of this experience, if one day I do live with a partner or have kids, I'm not going to be as bothered by the dishes in the sink or someone stomping around the house.

You can't really live an unexamined life in a housing situation where you have roommates who have to give each other feedback as part of working toward what you're trying to accomplish. You have to look inward and be able to take that feedback in order to work together. And you sharpen those communication and conflict resolution skills in intentional community because you won't be successful if you don't, but it does take more work and time and intention.

Communal living is also a good exercise in learning how to talk to people when you have your roommates' friends coming in and out of the house. When we're choosing our own friends, the default is to gravitate toward people who are more or less like us, even if we try to have a more expansive circle. The exposure to more diverse viewpoints and people you might never otherwise come across is a huge benefit.

What have you discovered about the intersection of identity and communal living in working with religious, ethnic, and racial minorities—and being a Black Jewish woman yourself?

I always felt very much like an outsider growing up in Seattle, where my family moved from Idaho partly because of anti-Semitism and racism. My mom's a white Jewish lady with two mixed-race kids. I didn't see a lot of people who looked like me. Early on, I had a sense that there was something about my background or my mom that was troubling to people.

When you feel different coming of age in the States, like a lot of minorities do, especially disenfranchised or targeted minorities, belonging is a feeling you really crave. I appreciate my differences now, but there's also something beautiful about being in a community where you feel a sense of equity and reciprocity. That just didn't exist for me before I went to Israel. Then, living in the Jewish community the way that I did in Moishe House made me feel—and still makes me feel—very whole.

People join Moishe House for a number of reasons. Some just join for the cheap rent, but some have experiences where it feels like a piece of their identity is filled that they wouldn't have filled otherwise. Communal living, for me, wasn't about discovering more about who I was. It was taking on a collective identity that I needed.

Where do you see the trajectory of communal living going in the next decade or so?

We're already starting to apply community-building skills people relied on in the past to help us create a more sustainable future, and I see that increasing. A lot of us are in this "sandwich generation" where we're raising young kids and taking care of elder parents. Because of this, I think these people in particular are going to be trending more toward unconventional housing solutions.

Especially in large metropolitan areas, there's a strong desire for communal living, whether for economic or social reasons. We haven't made dents in the loneliness epidemic. The need for connection and community is still very much present. With Moishe House, we're getting more applications than ever before and we can't pursue all of them even though we try to have as many houses as we can. People are also staying in the houses for longer. The demand and the desire are there.

Mem Global—and the Moishe House program—is, of course, one organization with one specific mission. Do you see gaps in the areas of communal living and community building that you feel could be filled by other people or organizations? Do you have any ideas for how we can start to fill them?

We get requests all the time to have Moishe Houses for seniors. I wish we could. My mom just turned eighty and she lives alone with a Life Alert that I monitor from the other side of the country. There are a lot of people like that, and elder care is a huge gap in this country.

The other gap is interfaith community. There's an organization called Abrahamic House, which has a Christian, a Muslim, and a Jewish person living together and celebrating holidays, and that's where I'm going for Passover this year. There are so many global problems right now, and something that's always on my mind is the divisions that exist between our faith traditions. We're always looking for a big viral moment or a rally to move the needle, but what really moves the needle are these deep interpersonal relationships that you work through when spending time with or living alongside others. I think it's a fabulous model that will have a deep effect not just on the people who live in the house but on those who go to the programs. It's a challenging but beautiful thing that can change people's perceptions of one another.

HELLO TO ALL THIS

Gabrielle Korn

As we moved in, I joked: "If I ever get fired, we can put my office on Airbnb." I should know better than to speak these things out loud.

There is a certain type of die-hard New Yorker who loves to make fun of the person who leaves for Los Angeles. Joan Didioning—the verb. Goodbye to all that, etcetera. The people who needed something more than the city could give, which in turn meant they were soft and boring. I was guilty of turning my nose up at those people too. For fourteen years, I lived around Manhattan and Queens and North Brooklyn and South Brooklyn, could navigate the subway with my eyes closed, and felt high off of the constant *Oh my god, hi how are you* of running into acquaintances almost everywhere I went, as though the city was just one inch big, its own community, where I felt I belonged.

I couldn't imagine ever actually living anywhere else but also couldn't imagine what it might feel like to not be exhausted and broke and cramped. Didion said it best: "I talk about how difficult it would be for us to 'afford' to live in New York right now, about how much 'space' we need. All I mean is that I was very young in New York, and that at some point the golden rhythm was broken, and I am not that young anymore."[1]

Like her, I was young in New York, and then I wasn't that young, but I was still there and I still really loved it. I was not planning on leaving the city, maybe not ever, but when Netflix descended from the heavens and offered to nearly triple my media salary and relocate me and my wife, Wallace, and our two dogs to LA in the middle of the pandemic, the question had answered itself. It was not the kind of job you say no to, not given the money nor what was happening to the industry where I'd been an editor for a decade. This felt like my way out.

Our new realtor directed us to Silver Lake, a place so teeming with other ex-New Yorkers that it almost sounded like a bit of a cliché, but it was also so beautiful, more beautiful than anywhere I ever thought I'd live: hot pink bougainvillea growing wild against the bright blue sky, mountains in the distance, that sort of thing. We found a little house that was the same square footage as our Brooklyn apartment, but it was a *house!* My tech salary meant we could afford to live in it. We painted the living room pink, the kitchen green, and spent probably too much money turning the junglelike garden into a tiny paradise. There was even a guest room with a separate entrance, and I turned it into my office. Heaven. As we moved in, I joked: "If I ever get fired, we can put my office on Airbnb."

I should know better than to speak these things out loud.

I made it almost a year before I lost the job that brought me to LA. I'd never been laid off before, though I'd certainly left jobs, and I couldn't stop repeating a certain version of the story to myself and others: *I moved across the country for a job I then lost.* I'd left my family and all my friends and favorite places and my routines for something that fell apart, and now I was stranded.

So, after a budget remodel, onto Airbnb the office went. We set the price at the lowest end of the spectrum for the neighborhood, not wanting to rip people off, and then sat back and watched. Within a few days, we started getting bookings. And then, before we knew it, the entire summer was booked.

We threw ourselves into hosting, opting not to hire a cleaning service but to do it ourselves to keep the money, since I wasn't sure what kind of job I wanted or could even get next. Cleaning the unit every few days was . . . deeply humbling, to say the least. People are disgusting. I could tell you detailed, lurid stories about guests who don't flush the toilet, or the person who bled on the curtains, but I'll spare you.

Soon we started to have repeat stays. In their reviews, people described our studio as their happy place. They wanted to come back, and a lot of them did. Although it wasn't a community in a traditional sense—we didn't have personal relationships with the guests—our home had become something meaningful to them and their lives. It wasn't just a place they stayed on a work trip (though it was also that). It was a place where they found respite. We had that in common. I began to feel an emotional connection to these strangers staying downstairs. I felt invested in their enjoyment and proud that my home could provide it.

The income from the Airbnb was, all of a sudden, paying for the mortgage. This meant I didn't have to get another nine-to-five job and could pivot to writing full-time, which never felt possible before, while Wallace could continue to paint commissions for private clients. But I didn't want to be a landlord. Ideologically, I felt the bulk of my income shouldn't come from tenants; even though it was amazing, I was conflicted about the politics. LA is facing a housing shortage and many point to Airbnbs as the problem. I don't think that's always the case—our studio is too small for anyone to live in as a primary residence, so we wouldn't be able to get a long-term tenant—but I understood the problems even as I benefited.

To offset some of these concerns, we decided to also use the studio for good. We started inviting writers and artists to stay for free for a few nights every month, a little mini residency for those who couldn't afford to leave their lives for weeks at a time, something traditional residencies typically require. I put the call out on social media and was flooded with applicants. We prioritized people we didn't know but made time for our friends to visit too. Guests would come for three or four days and hole up downstairs. We'd sometimes catch glimpses of them in the window, curled into their work for days.

Eventually we gave our project a name—The Pink Door Artist and Writer Residency—and a proper application process. Now every time we open up for applications, we get dozens. I've met all kinds of authors through the program, from established creatives that I'm a personal fan of to writers working on their debuts. There's a guestbook I ask people to sign, and most take up at least a full page describing their experiences in the studio, sharing advice and tips for the next resident.

Not everyone wants to hang out with us when they come for the residency—which is fine, they're here to work—but others want to go on walks with me or grab coffee. We talk about publishing, about what they're working on, about the state of the world and the role of art in it. And then, we stay in touch. We support each other's projects as they are released into the world. There's an ongoing and irreplaceable connection that's formed after someone stays in our house.

Initially it was hard to make friends in LA, to find community in a city that bends toward the entertainment industry. But through the residency, and the writers and artists we met simply by announcing it, I've started to feel as though I have a place here. Sometimes, I meet people who have already heard about the residency, who learned about it before they knew who I was. It's become something bigger than us.

There is a thriving literary scene in LA, but like anything, it's hard to break into. At first, I'd show up to book events not knowing anyone and leave without having managed to even say hi to a single person. I'd watch on Instagram as local authors supported each other, spent time together, participated in community together. I realized I couldn't be part of it simply by virtue of wanting to.

By opening up our home to strangers, we also opened a door to the scene in general. Once I had a literary publicist stay for two weeks, and she hosted a party for writers in our backyard. We'd never had so many strangers over before, and it resembled a distinctly LA cultural moment not unlike what Didion cultivated: we were inviting people into our lives. At that party, I met the bookseller from the bookstore that would later host my own novel launch, and local writers who've remained friends. These are the people I recognize at book events now, whose work I'm always excited to talk about and help elevate. Often, now, they even ask me to host those events with them. With some of the authors I've met here, I formed a writing group, and we've committed to meeting once a week, taking turns workshopping each other's drafts. It's a little like group therapy and even more like family.

None of this—the residencies and resulting community, the rental income—would have happened if I hadn't moved here and then lost my job. So the *I moved across the country for a job I then lost* narrative is really only one way of looking at things. The other way is: my time in New York had expired, and a job with relocation benefits came along at the perfect time. It afforded me the immense privilege of buying a house in a nice neighborhood, and now I get to be here, even without that job.

I *get* to be here. Here, in LA, a place where you can actually live off of freelance work, even without a trust fund, where I can take calls in the morning and then run around the reservoir and make a big salad with gorgeous produce and then clean the Airbnb for the next guest and then write an essay and go to bed early and still pay my bills.

I'm not sure if we'll be renting out the studio forever—at some point, it would be nice to have an extra bedroom and bathroom, and hopefully, we won't always be so strapped for cash—although I don't want to have to give up the residency program, either. I like to think long-term, but the nature of being a full-time creative doesn't really lend itself to that, and I'm trying to make peace with it. We'll do the residency as long as we're renting out that space. And maybe, if someday we don't need to rent the space anymore, we can still find a way to host writers and artists.

Through this transition, my home has become something more than just where I live. It's part of my livelihood and it connects me to the greater artistic community—the kind of community that had buzzed around me in my New York life, that I wasn't sure I would ever be able to recreate elsewhere. It has a different energy than the one in New York, though; it's more intimate. It's driving through the narrow, winding hills to go to people's homes for dinner and drinking orange wine in their living rooms surrounded by their books and art and dogs instead of taking the subway to the bar for an overpriced drink after work. At this point, I wouldn't have it any other way.

Q&A *with* HANK GAMEL *and* FRAN BIEDERMAN

Maybe the whole lesson is we need to challenge ourselves more in terms of our thought process and embrace doing things differently.

In 2014, Hank Gamel became executive director of Hope Meadows, an intergenerational neighborhood that intentionally brought together seniors and families adopting children in foster care. It was the first of its kind in the United States.[1]

For twenty years, Hope Meadows, located on a former US Air Force base in Rantoul, Illinois, had offered free housing, a stipend, and benefits to foster and adoptive parents, as well as low-market rent to seniors who volunteered six hours a week in the community. Fran Biederman and her husband were the first seniors to move into Hope Meadows, in 1994. Now widowed and in her nineties, Fran has found that living in the neighborhood among the forty families, twenty-five kids, and thirty seniors is still ideal. And yet, even as the Hope Meadows model has led to the development of similar communities across the country, it hasn't been without difficulties.

When Hank, now in his sixties, took over as executive director, Hope Meadows had been struggling financially for much of its second decade. A retired police officer, Hank was active in developing alternate models of policing during his time on the force and sought to bring his experience to the community. Its board of directors had to make hard choices, charging rent to families who had previously lived for free and pivoting to include a broader range of residents. There aren't as many community programs as there once were—in the past, there was bicycle repair, after-school education, a community garden, potlucks, and museum field trips—but residents still have access to a food bank, weekly bingo, and service projects. Through it all, Hank and Fran believe Hope Meadows has retained its original spirit, with neighbors going out of their way to help one another even in the absence of more formal community programming, and they shared what we can learn from its successes and challenges.

How has Hope Meadows evolved over the last thirty years?

HG: When Hope Meadows began, there were fifty-one thousand kids every year going into foster care in Illinois, and they spent nearly three years there before adoption.[2] The goal of Hope Meadows was permanent adoption for children in foster care. The idea of adding seniors to the community came up because of the footprint of the property, which was three times more than they were originally seeking. I think what propelled it to get so much attention in that first decade was that it really mirrored the African proverb "It takes a village to raise a child," because every child that lived there had a neighborhood of surrogate grandparents.

One of my first meetings as a board member in the year before I became executive director was a community meeting where the board explained that they could no longer provide free housing or healthcare and IRA benefits for foster parents. The original state grants that provided the majority of the funds were foster care grants, but in the 1990s, several federal acts were passed to reduce the timeline for kids in foster care. By 2013, the numbers had gone down to fifteen thousand kids a year going into foster care in Illinois and the timeline went from almost three years to approximately one year before adoption. And that progress, while wonderful for timely, permanent adoptions, meant less funding for Hope Meadows.

It was proposed that we gradually implement a stair-step increase of rent and also close the foster care license. The intent was to still accept and offer a supportive community to foster and adoptive families and to charge a reduced rent but not to be the provider of future adoption services, which was the largest cost. It was hard to say we're going to have to do something that nobody wants or likes, which is why it took a decade to address it, but it passed, although I regret not verbalizing my concerns about what struck me as a rather drastic change. We had a few foster and adoptive families move in after that, but the masses never really followed. It wasn't the same without the allure of free housing.

But we found new ways to make use of the space. It was always an intergenerational neighborhood, and we've accommodated several three- and four-generation families within the houses that have six or eight bedrooms. We also have duplexes, and there are some families where Mom and Grandma live on one side and the adult children live on the other side with their kids.

Why did you decide to move to Hope Meadows?

FB: My husband, Bill, was on disability, and he was just hanging around the house doing nothing. I saw an ad in the paper about Hope, and the house we were living in was going to be sold. I applied, and we were accepted. I was still working full-time as a secretary for the National Council of Teachers of English. Bill loved kids and it got him out of the house. It was mainly for him, because he needed it, and it worked very well.

It was a fabulous program, as far as I'm concerned—one of the best programs I could see around helping kids and parents. I went to some of the kids' adoptions, and they were so pleased that someone was going to be their mom and dad. All the kids called us Grandma and Grandpa. You had to be here to really appreciate what we had.

What are some of the ways that you've witnessed neighbors helping one another over the years?

HG: We've had a few people who grew up here as adoptees choose to come back and live here as adults for the familiar and supportive community. There's a lot of natural neighbor interactions that always happened, and they're still happening. During the height of the pandemic, one of the seniors who used to do after-school education tutored their neighbor's two boys. Then there's one lady in her eighties whose neighbor watched out for her and picked up her mail. The older woman recently had to go to a skilled living facility and her next of kin are holding garage sales to get rid of items from her house. Her next-door neighbor has been out there every day with the family trying to help them sell things. Nobody asked her to do that. She just cares about her neighbor. And then there's Fran and Chari.

FB: My neighbor Chari, who lives on the other side of my duplex, does most things by herself, unless she thinks she can be helpful in some way to another person. She's single and she has three adult children, but they all live far away. She doesn't like cloudy days, and I know when she doesn't want to be bothered; I can just tell. But she's right there to do anything for me, and I will do the same for her. Since she's on a fixed income, I send her notices of when they have food drives and I told her where she could apply for help with utilities. She always wants to take me to the doctor. We say good morning and good night, and she'll either call me or text me every day. I'll let her know everything's okay, and she'll do the same. Our bathrooms connect, and we can open our medicine cabinets and have a conversation. She's a very good neighbor and a very good person. In fact, we just came back from going out to breakfast this morning. Chari loves to drive, and we've been North, South, East, and West. Just wake up one morning, decide to go to breakfast, and end up thirty miles away. It's good for me and it's good for her because we both get out.

What have seniors and foster families reported to be their favorite parts of living in this community?

HG: It can be pretty stressful raising a family of foster kids, and I've heard from more than one parent that it was so nice to have so many people willing to help. It was easy to call a neighbor at 8 p.m. and say you needed a hand. They would say, "Send the kids over here," and the kids would walk next door and spend the night there. There was one lady who used to have kids over to her place to make pancakes on Saturday mornings.

For the seniors, it was and is very supportive. Someone is always taking someone to a doctor's appointment, which is important because not everyone drives. And the people who drive are happy to do this for their neighbor. In the past, many of the older kids would do things for their senior neighbors, like mow their lawn or help them carry their grocery bags. There was a regular, consistent behavior of neighbors helping neighbors and we're continuing to see that.

When new people move in now, they're not required to do service hours, but they hear about the history of the place, and they see everyone being nice and helpful, and they start doing it themselves. That's what people tend to appreciate about the community, as well as a sense of belonging or acceptance.

FB: My husband was the one who spent most of the time with the kids, outside of my volunteer hours, since I worked full-time. The kids helped Bill just by being there. Everybody thought he was healthy, but he had heart disease and some other problems. He had a chance to get acquainted with the kids, and they felt comfortable enough to ask about his health.

He'd be sitting in the carport with another neighbor, and kids would just come up and talk to him. He loved when they came over and he played games with them. There was this one little girl who lived across the street, and she used to do cartwheels from her house to our house. Then she'd want ramen noodles, so he'd go in the house and cook her ramen noodles. He repaired all of the tricycles and bikes for the kids too, and one boy would come by every day wanting something else done to his bike. Hope Meadows was the best medicine for Bill. And even though the kids spent more time with him, I did get something out of it. I attended all their events, and I always told them they were welcome at my house anytime.

It was great for the kids too. My neighbor and I used to take walks, and one time this little Black boy came up and said, "Hi Grandma Fran, hi Grandma Irene." He had a biological cousin visiting him who said, "They're not your grandmas." And he looked at her and answered, "They're my Hope grandmas!" That's just how it worked.

What do you feel is important to talk about when we consider putting systems in place to serve seniors and families?

HG: Long-term planning. I learned years ago that when you make a purchase of something new, that's a good time to ask what the life cycle is and how you're going to replace it at the end of its life cycle. In the beginning of Hope Meadows, I think they were so eager and committed to doing something different, and it was so successful initially, that I'm not sure anyone thought about what's going to happen twenty to thirty years from now. We know the roofs aren't going to last forever and we have to be putting money aside for that, but we have no capital budget and not many opportunities for the type of assistance that we really need. With seniors, they should have been asking what kind of help people are going to require in the future because the majority of our structures have two flights of stairs. What are we going to do as people have more falls and assistive care becomes a necessity? I'm pursuing a model where we could have somebody come out periodically and offer in-home services, especially to those who are low income, but we have no funding to contract such services.

How can organizations, existing social services, and even everyday people help support models like Hope Meadows?

HG: Grants are one essential thing, as well as donations. We could also always use help from tradespeople. For a few years, we had a grant in partnership with our local high school and Habitat for Humanity, in which high school students would do repairs to the units at Hope Meadows. The kids were taught in home repair and similar trades courses—this is how you put up drywall, this is how you put a light in the ceiling—and then got credit for receiving training in an environment that ultimately benefited others, rather than just in a makeshift shop. It lasted for more than three years.

We would also be happy to host models, demonstrations, and pilot projects. We have twenty-two acres of grass and we'd love to have a solar field or something like that if an organization wanted to do it for a demonstration. It's just that start-up, that capital, that we're lacking. Finally, we have had some mutually beneficial collaborations with organizations providing on-site youth services, as well as elder services, although the lack of public transit in our region complicates such partnerships.

You hear almost every day in the national news about the housing shortage, particularly for people who are not high income. We are basically a provider of affordable housing, and we could use some funding to continue our work and upgrade to provide better housing. My hope is that as the need and the dialogue eventually come to fruition, we might be able to do much more with some kind of funding mechanism.

And how can broadening our conception of housing by turning away from single-family households, as well as leaning more into community, address some of the challenges we face with the loneliness epidemic, housing crisis, and aging population? How might it allow at least some of us to experience more joy?

HG: Multipurpose housing that could accommodate a changing society could solve a lot of problems. I've always wanted to think creatively to tie Hope Meadows to what our contemporary societal problems are and to be adaptable to whatever they become. Our seniors at Hope Meadows have never wanted to be segregated. As people age, they perk up when younger people come around. Also, more young adults are still living with their parents because of economic inequality and the cost of housing, and it would be great to have more housing structures that accommodate them.

Maybe the whole lesson is we need to challenge ourselves more in terms of our thought process and embrace doing things differently, with research and long-term planning. When I think back to 1994, it was a pretty unconventional idea to build a big neighborhood foster home on an old air force base. It raised some eyebrows. But it was worth taking a chance.

THE MYTH OF STABLE GROUND

Amanda E. Machado

Being "grounded" requires more than the simplicity of staying in one place, or building one home. It requires the more difficult thing: holding all the complexity of what it takes to exist within a constantly unstable and unjust world.

In the beginning, my home was mostly water. A necessary marsh that protected the land around it from flooding, cleansed the land of poison, purified the air. The Ohlone people who lived here knew we needed wetlands to keep the earth in balance, and so they stewarded this marshland for over ten thousand years.

Two hundred years ago, my home became a landfill. After killing and enslaving the Ohlone people throughout this region, colonizers drained the wetlands and covered them in trash. The US government passed the Swamp Land Act, which made it easier for people to claim wetlands as their own property if they turned them into dry land for agricultural purposes.[1] Trash and any spare items were used to make the ground firm enough for development. They called this process "reclamation." D, my landlord, says when he's digging through the dirt, he sometimes finds remnants in our backyard: bottles and tin cans from the 1800s, piles of historical garbage. Later, this unstable ground—far more susceptible to damage during earthquakes—became the place to house Black and immigrant workers, the red-lined area for folks of color not allowed to live in other parts of the city.

Forty years ago, D was born in this home. His great-great-grandmother migrated with her family from Texas to California after they, like many Black families, lost their land through racist policies enacted after slavery. His grandparents bought this home in Oakland in 1958 and raised their seven children here. Over time, the family managed to buy two houses across the street, a few on the next block over. The goal was a house for every child, a place where each of them could settle down.

Today, we live on the same block as two of D's aunts and his grandmother, his uncle lives a few streets away, and other family members are scattered within a five-block radius of us. D lives a few miles east. When my housemates and I move in, we like that this block of Oakland still has mostly people of color, like us. We like that we'll be paying rent to a Black family who has lived in this area for almost one hundred years. We tell ourselves it feels better to give our money to D's family, rather than the gigantic exploitative management companies we used to pay with our previous housing, the same companies who evicted so many people during the pandemic. We tell ourselves rent can be some small form of repairing things.

Growing up in Florida, after school I would often ride my bike toward the rich neighborhood—the one with all the waterfront houses. I liked biking in late evening, seeing the sun set on the water, making the waves look like glass. By dusk, I'd watch the warm golden lamps turn on in the windows of each house, the open curtains allowing just a quick glimpse of what was inside: cozy dens filled with books, families sitting down to dinner on long, elegant tables.

I daydreamed about buying one of these houses one day: a house with a wraparound front porch and a large oak tree or an oval-shaped window over the second-floor staircase. It seemed impossible for anyone to feel stressed or unhappy when living in a house like that, one so meticulously designed to evoke a sense of ease. I imagined the calm pleasure the families living in those houses must experience: lavish holiday dinners by the fireplace, summers tanning by the dock after an afternoon of jet skiing, evenings snacking on fruit beneath the shade of the porch. As a kid, I still believed that storybook houses inherently could create a storybook life. I believed that the ease I wanted for myself could be obtained by just buying one of those houses on the water, getting access to their kind of peace.

My grandmother struggled all her life to have a house. For years, she moved from place to place with her children, trying to escape my abusive grandfather, staying anywhere and with anyone who could offer her and her children somewhere to sleep. She crossed the border continuing to search for home and struggled again—sometimes living in a camper parked on the side of the road, sometimes living in the back of her herbalist store to save on rent, sometimes getting evicted when she couldn't keep up with the rising rent.

Decades later, my grandmother died living in her own house, a house her children bought for her, a fact that sometimes feels like triumph after everything she experienced. Like D's family, my mother also hoped to buy a house for each member of our family. "Everyone needs a home they know they can come back to," she used to say. "Just in case."

When D's family first moved into this house, the neighborhood was known as the Harlem of the West Coast. Stars like Ray Charles, Jimi Hendrix, Stevie Wonder, and Aretha Franklin all performed at the Continental Club, just blocks from our front door. Black-owned businesses, night clubs, and cafes were bustling everywhere.

After the 1950s, everything changed. The city built a freeway right down the middle of the neighborhood—something they could never get away with in wealthier white areas. Then they built the Oakland Post Office and the metro station on the busiest street, lined with shops and cafes. The city claimed eminent domain, taking private properties for public use and displacing over five thousand families. The businesses had to leave, the cafes closed down. Pollution here became four times higher than in wealthier areas of the city. A few years ago, doctors discovered D's niece had elevated levels of lead in her body, after regularly playing in the backyard of this house.

According to a study by the Alameda County Health Department, the life expectancy of a person in this neighborhood now is more than twelve years below a person living up in the Oakland Hills.[2]

I came to Oakland after years of bouncing around semi-nomadically from different cities in the US and abroad. I had let go of the dream of the storybook house for a while, after ending a relationship with a wealthy white man who came the closest in my life to providing it. Loving someone involved in family conversations about trust funds, inheritance taxes, and properties worth millions, I slowly became skeptical that I could actually live a life in adherence to this kind of capitalistic thriving. I saw more clearly what "storybook lives" actually entailed, what sacrifices of self they often required: homogenous social circles comprised mostly of Ivy League graduates, Wall Street bankers, and McKinsey consultants. Dinner conversations with tempered politics, a seemingly understood agreement to never mention radical change. An overall ambiance to life that felt detached from reality. I began to rethink whether that kind of home was worth it.

Instead, I traveled abroad, with only what could fit in my suitcase, and for years, I rarely spent more than three months in the same place. I explored the notion of home as a thing we could carry with us, something not based on any external, material structure, but on an internal sense of stability.

During a brief time living in Havana, Cuba, I read *Giovanni's Room*, in which James Baldwin wrote, "Perhaps home is not a place, but an irrevocable condition."[3] I thought about this quote all the time—how I could create a sense of home inside myself that felt irrevocable, that felt protected and safe and mine.

"Home isn't a place; it's a *feeling*," many fellow traveling expats I'd meet would say. I felt this during that period of my life—the unique liberation of learning to belong in a variety of conditions and environments, the freedom of feeling an abundant sense of home.

But the older I got, the more the desire came back. After so much movement, I began wanting at least one actual physical space where I could feel at ease. I found myself thinking again about what my mother used to say: everyone, at some point, wants a home they can come back to.

I moved to Oakland seeking less travel and more home. But it didn't take long to notice how the city's history of housing injustice continued: the obscenely inequitable rents, the unjust evictions, the constant calls from government officials to criminalize those who were unhoused while disregarding the need for affordable housing. The people in charge of the land were almost always white families, or white-led property management companies. Since I couldn't afford a one bedroom on a writer's salary, I fell into the long-held Bay Area tradition of communal housing, and still noticed the same pattern: most of the co-ops I lived in or knew by association were owned or run by white folks. I thought back to my childhood bike rides through wealthy white neighborhoods, my former relationship with that wealthy white partner who wanted to settle down, the shortcut to home and stability that I had declined. Too often, home still seemed to require the power and access of white folks. There were too few examples of how to build it any other way.

A few months later, some friends and I searched Craigslist and found D's house.

In the three years I have lived here, my housemates and I have made specific intentions: First, we only consider queer and trans people of color as housemates. We wanted a space that felt like rest when it came to issues of those identities. A space where we didn't have to tend to white cis straight comfort—particularly in the language we used around race, gender, and sexuality—as we often had to once we left the house.

Second, we wanted to create a vibe within the house that felt closer to what we think of as family—shopping at Costco together, giving each other rides to the airport, visiting three grocery stores the day before a holiday meal searching for the right ingredients—but queerer than any of our families ever allowed us to be. There is something healing about getting a chance to redo these rituals from my childhood now with a celebration of queerness I never had in my own home. It is also remarkably liberating to create entirely new rituals that our own families may have never even imagined, or that were colonized out of us. On full moons, we often make a fire in the backyard and toss our written intentions for the month into the flame. For my birthday, we picked Mexican marigold from a bush on a nearby sidewalk and gave each other limpias. On Mother's Day—a troubled holiday for many queer folks—we have a tradition to spend the day drinking champagne and watching gay TV. Some days, living here feels like a tiny slice of queer, POC utopia, like an insulated world we can hibernate in each day, before stepping out into a more hostile world outside.

We also try to make housing decisions that invest in the world we want outside the house. We pay a Shuumi Land Tax, a calculated percentage of our rent that we automatically give to the Indigenous-led land trust in the area.[4] We try to only buy house supplies and cleaning products that aren't on the Palestinian Boycott, Divest, and Sanctions list. We have an agreement that outside of dire emergencies, we don't call the cops.

Of course, we're far from perfect. Sharing queer and POC identities does not automatically mean there aren't other differences that can cause tensions. Just because we've freed ourselves from certain conflicts in the home, like tending to white fragility or getting shamed for our sexuality, doesn't mean we've freed ourselves from conflict all together. And even in a house owned and lived in by people of color, we still grapple with our role as POC gentrifiers and transplants, and what really feels like the best way to contribute to this city versus taking something of it away.

But perhaps the core belief we all share in this house is that home, like everything, must be political, because home is the root of what oppression takes away.

In her essay "Tracing Harriet Tubman's Steps," Jehan Roberson argues that for Black Americans after slavery, "to be in community and to make yourself known was revolutionary, a radically subversive act towards slavery, to stake a claim on home, to not make yourself a migrant, or a 'foreigner.'"[5]

As a non-Black person of color, this definition of home still resonates—home as a resistance toward a system that has thrived by making Black, Indigenous, and people of color feel constantly displaced. Perhaps this, too, is what I wanted from the house: to feel entitled to stake a claim on home. A space where home could be both an irrevocable condition and an actual place where we can make ourselves known.

The questions I am still asking: What is a home outside of heteronormative partnership, and without biological children? What is a home that doesn't displace someone else's home? If we climb the ladder of US capitalism to become landlords, what is our responsibility to do next? What is a home that does not replicate capitalist, colonialist, white supremacist dynamics that often become entangled in our notions of "settling down"?

I have no role models for what I necessarily want to build. I had no storybooks written about houses like ours. Since none of the old rules apply, most of the time we're all making it up as we go.

Meanwhile, I am realizing now how any home cannot necessarily assure that anything stays stable and can create different burdens. Financially, it's unclear whether any of us can manage to afford this place much longer. PG&E, the private monopoly that provides gas and electricity for northern California, has increased rates by 54 percent since 2020, after they had to pay over $1 billion in civil penalties for starting some of California's worst wildfires.[6] D still grapples with how to negotiate raising rent in order to meet the rising utilities and maintenance costs, while also keeping it sustainable for a group of queer POC artists.

All over the country, Black families face similar problems. On the islands off the coast of the Carolinas, Black families struggle to hold on to their generational land because of rising property taxes. After hurricanes, floods, and other natural disasters, Black families often don't qualify for government assistance because their land was passed down for generations through a family without an official deed.[7] And, amidst all the obstacles created by our housing systems, family trauma complicates everything too. D admits that his family members quarrel about decisions surrounding the houses they jointly own. The family members who live next door to each other aren't necessarily as emotionally close as they are geographically. And, in my family, despite my mother's words about home, once I came out as queer, our relationship became estranged, and we've gone years without speaking. I haven't visited the house my family owns and lives in for years.

I know through all these stories that houses can create freedom and also can become traps, that even once we obtain the safety of a home, the systems and culture we live in make that sense of safety impossible to maintain, and it feels constantly at risk. I know that a family can work all their lives to buy a house that will not necessarily feel like a safe place to come back to. I know that having a house does not necessarily guarantee the sense of rest I've always searched for.

In our house in Oakland, we struggle with how often folks move in and out, for work or school or changing finances or other shifting needs. To live here, we have to accept that we're living in something as fluid as our queer and trans lives.

In her essay "Nadie la tiene: Land, Ecology and Nationalism," Puerto Rican writer Aurora Levins Morales describes the myth of stable ground.[8] She explains that five tons of soil each year leave every acre of land throughout the US, "blown by wind across property lines and fences, municipalities and national borders . . . Just as the air we breathe has been breathed by millions of others first . . . so the land itself migrates."

Similarly, in her essay "Grounded," Anishinaabe writer Aubrey Streit Krug reminds us that "ground overflows boundaries," that "ground both is and isn't solid, so grounded both is and isn't a stable state."[9] To Krug, this signifies that being "grounded" must mean more than just "obedience to gravity." It requires more than the simplicity of staying in one place or building one home. It requires the more difficult thing: holding all the complexity of what it takes to exist within a constantly unstable and unjust world.

Reading this, I reflect on all the superficial ways that humans try to "settle down," how we often chase arbitrary milestones that make us believe we've achieved the groundedness we want. I think about my childhood biking around rich neighborhoods, my naive trust in the systems that could create my storybook house and storybook life, my foolish belief that obedience to gravity in that corner of the world could somehow solve everything. I grieve the part of me that hoped home could be simpler. I grieve how complicated it all turned out to be, that home couldn't necessarily be found in the places I thought.

A commitment to fluidity, in all of its freedom—and even in its genuine reflection of earth and nature and life—can also sometimes feel like a commitment to a kind of endurance I'm not always sure I have. It is far easier to believe that the ground won't move, that the migration is over, that there is an actual place to reach and rest.

This is all to say: living in this house, I have felt more at ease and at home with myself than anywhere else I have in the world. And the house, the land, is changing, will always change, will always move. That's its commitment too.

In the beginning, this land was swamp, then landfill, then a Black family's new home. And now we're here, knowing that the land and soil will keep transforming but wanting a future where oppression is no longer the main force transforming it.

In that future, there are no landlords. There is no such thing as an eminent domain. In the future, this land is returned to the Ohlone people, and maybe the swamps and the marshlands come back.

In the future, children play in backyards that don't have lead, and no one has a memory of a grandmother who ever had to roam the streets with her children, trying to find a place to sleep. In the future, my mother's wish comes true for every person, and for the two of us: we all have a home to come back to.

Until then, as I read the essays by Krug and Levins Morales, there is relief in this idea that even the soil beneath our feet is inherently unstable, that we are not the only ones displaced, that the dirt, too, gets lost and blown in wrong directions, and travels and moves all the time. There's relief in the idea that as queer people of color, our lineage of displacement perhaps makes us more prepared and adaptive to this dynamic, that we've become experts at creating stability on migrating land. We've had to practice this different kind of groundedness all our lives. The sense of home I've found with queer people of color comes from that practice. We're a community of people who know how to take care of each other amidst the volatile change around us. People committed to the "irrevocable condition" of loving each other even amidst impossible circumstances. As queer people of color, we know that home often is something we have to build from scratch, and so we rebuild it, over and over again.

ENOUGH IS AS GOOD AS A FEAST

Kim Stanley Robinson

I found that the peace and quiet of the evenings, and the sight of so many faces of known friends and acquaintances, all gathered so casually, combined to create a particular pleasure that never went away.

I've lived in a small alternative community for the past twenty-seven years. It's not that alternative, really just a suburban subdivision near the west edge of Davis, California, called Village Homes. Eighty-five acres of tomato fields were developed in the late 1970s, with the idea of tweaking the usual template of American postwar suburbia to something more like a European village from an older era. Streets were made as dead-ended lanes, walking paths ran between fenceless common areas, and swales were cut into the land to capture water in the rainy season and direct it back down into the ground. Residents own their own homes and usually have a small private courtyard space, but otherwise, the land is owned communally by all homeowners, and decisions about land use are made by a small volunteer government with town hall voting. Organic gardening space is available to all who want it, and the landscaping is mostly edible in the form of fruit and nut trees. The community is anchored by a small restaurant, a set of offices for rent, a swimming pool, and crucially, a preschool daycare center that rents the community center during weekdays. Energy use is about 40 percent of typical suburban use, and about eight hundred to a thousand people live here, so it is neither very energy efficient nor very densely populated.[1] Taken all in all, it's not paradise or utopia or the housing solution to the world's ills, but it is nice, and for me, it has proved the idea that urban design influences social reality, and that infrastructure helps to determine social and human relations.

Thus Village Homes, and because it's residential, there is a food angle to it, including that social aspect of food we sometimes call a feast.

The crucial element in our social life, as I said, was the preschool in the community center. We've never met all the people in the village, but we did meet the parents of the kids that our kids were playing with at school. The pool next to the community center and the big green flanking it were obvious places to go after picking up the kids, and as the kids continued to play together, the parents got to know each other. Thus grew some of the closest relationships of our life, those family-by-affinity relationships that I think were common in older forms of village life. It was easy and felt natural, and it's lasted beyond the time of the children growing up. And as part of that, we often ate together.

In those years, a gazebo at the south end of the big green served as a meeting place for potluck dinners. For many years we met there on Thursdays, spring through fall. In the long evenings people brought out vegetarian dishes, which often included food grown in our gardens. The kids ate and played on the big green while the parents ate and talked. The variety of dishes was wonderful, and I found the ease with which such quality dining and socializing could be created remarkable. Having grown up in the atomized standard American suburbia of the 1950s, consisting of nuclear families each tucked into their own mini castle, I was perpetually amazed that such little adjustments in form could lead to such big improvements in content.

I found that the peace and quiet of the evenings, and the sight of so many faces of known friends and acquaintances, all gathered so casually, combined to create a particular pleasure that never went away. Ease and unpretentiousness were very important to that feeling. Maybe one aspect of the commons that we don't know enough about to miss, having lived our lives without a commons, is that lack of structure and leadership. This was brought home to me by the way we used to harvest the village's almond trees, which grew in a three-tree strip along the street bordering our village. On harvest day a mechanical shaker like a small tractor was hired to visit, and as its operator drove from tree to tree, we moved big canvas sheets ahead of him, spreading them under the trees. Then he would clamp their trunks with his device's clawed arm, and it would shake down the almonds in a brief violent shivering, and when the almonds were all down, we would pull the sheets over to the street and dump the almonds into the gutter, where they could be easily swept into big burlap bags and later transferred to a long carport roof for drying in the sun. All this was done with no leadership, and even no organization; people just did what they wanted to. That self-organizing got the job done as efficiently, or maybe more efficiently, than if someone had been directing us. This felt wonderful. It felt ancient. It was harvesting, or gleaning, and it was palpable in our brains and bodies that we had evolved to do such things. We were social primates doing a social primate thing. The experience made me feel sure that vast parts of our brain still lie in wait, ready for moments like that one.

The potluck meals felt like that too. They were not feasts in the sense the word usually evokes; they were social, like feasts are, but they did not involve an excess of food. Quite often there wasn't even enough food, and over time, we had to adjust and bring a little more to make sure everyone got fed. But "enough is as good as a feast." This is an ancient English saying; it appears in the first few pages of *Bartlett's Familiar Quotations*, authored by the great anonymous.[2] It's worth pondering that phrase for a long time. Hungry people invented that phrase. It's not a capitalist sentiment; in fact, it reverses capitalist logic, but it could become part of a postcapitalist structure of feeling. The brain and body feel it well. One could even add to it, now, the medical news that not only is enough as good as a feast, it's better than a feast—as a feast is too much, by definition, and will make you sick, especially if you feast every day, as capitalism urges you to do. So as a working axiom for going forward, and finding a way to get in proper synch with our biosphere, even with all the eight billion people alive, and all the wild creatures too, it seems to me a crucial thing to keep in mind. Enough is as good as a feast—or better. And that's a good thing.

Now that the kids have grown up and moved away, our potluck in the village has stopped happening. Other potlucks in the village still fill the two greens on different nights; these may be focused on kids, or on particular common areas, or friendship groups within the village. I always like seeing them. For us, the potlucks served their purpose in their time. Maybe we'll revive them some day, those of us who still live here. Whether or not we do, it was a beautiful act of social creation—a result of living with a commons, rearing the kids together, and thinking socially and creatively. We were lucky.

PART III

BEYOND HOUSING

THE SHARED SECRET OF OUR LIVES

Simone Gorrindo

I needed that reliable, sturdy feeling of home I'd spent my whole life longing for, and she gave it to me, freely and without condition.

Nine days after I married my husband in a New York City courthouse, he left for boot camp. While he trained at bases across the country over the next year, I stayed in our four-hundred-square-foot apartment, eating frozen dinners for one. I'd spent a decade in New York, so I had a world of friends and colleagues, a job as an editor that I'd clawed my way into after years of waitressing. And yet, the year he was away was the loneliest year of my life. Everyone in New York was so *busy*, pressed against subway doors on crowded commutes to midtown offices, catching up on errands and quality time with spouses over the weekends. Some long weekends, the only people I spoke to were the two men who spent their days on my stoop listening to Bill Withers on a giant boom box. The lonelier I became, the more I secluded myself. New York was a restless sea and I'd lost my anchor, so I decided to let myself drift alone. In part, I did this because I knew my life was about to transform, and that I couldn't take anything of the world I'd built in New York—my career, my friends—on the journey.

The moment Andrew returned from training, a huge green rucksack in his hands, I felt all the tension in my body release, realizing only then just how much I'd been carrying—on my cold morning treks to the subway, in my fitful sleep in our half-empty bed, on our loveseat watching old episodes of *Veronica Mars* alone. I couldn't wait to walk to the northern edge of Central Park where Andrew had asked me to marry him, to eat breakfast together at the short-order diner beneath our apartment, the bacon so hot it melted the Styrofoam plates. But seeing him again, his hair shorter at the sides, his frame leaner, brought a fresh sadness. I was staring down the barrel of an even lonelier year ahead. We were moving, immediately, to our first duty station in Columbus, Georgia, where I knew no one. I had never been south of the Mason-Dixon line. I didn't have a driver's license. And two weeks after we got there, Andrew would be deploying to Afghanistan. I thought the previous year had been lonely? Well, I hadn't seen anything yet.

I had been vehemently against Andrew joining the Army. My parents had raised me on Vietnam protest songs, and I had marched against the invasion of Iraq. But after two years of discussions and months of visits to a couples' therapist, I decided, as the song goes, that *I'd rather live in his world than live without him in mine*. After he returned from boot camp, Andrew and I packed up our tiny apartment, and drove a U-Haul seventeen hours south to our new home, a little brick house fifteen minutes from base. The sun was just beginning to set when we arrived. As I surveyed the weedy lawn of the rental and took in the dead quiet of the street, my chest tightened. In that moment, I did not exactly regret my decision to marry Andrew, but I wondered how on earth I was going to live with it.

Within minutes, a slender woman with long chestnut hair appeared at the end of our driveway, as though we had summoned her. Her name, she told me eagerly as she took a box out of the U-Haul and rushed it to our stoop, was Rachel. Her husband had just gone through training with Andrew and was also deploying in two weeks. She was as new to this world as I was.

That same night, she brought us homemade chocolate chip cookies, still warm beneath the Saran Wrap. I told her that never, in all my years living in New York, had anyone baked me cookies.

"Well, your arrival is an event!" she said, smiling. "I've been across the street for two weeks." There was a faint desperation to her sweetness—a desperation I recognized because I'd been living with some version of it for the last year. Mine, though, had not made me sweet or eager like hers had. Andrew, the steadiest person I knew, had agreed to love me through sickness and health, and then, he left. I had been nursing that wound alone, afraid to rely on anyone but myself.

I took the cookies gratefully.

My childhood was not a recipe for belonging: my mother drank, my parents fought for years before finally divorcing, and my family struggled financially in one of California's richest counties. Abstractly, I understood what people meant when they said the word "home," but I wondered what it actually felt like. Dropping your keys on the entryway table after a long day? The relief of sitting down when your whole body ached? It had to be more than that, I knew, and whatever that was, I wanted it, badly. But I had no idea how to find it.

When I was seventeen, I dropped out of high school and moved to New York City, attending college through a program that didn't require a GED. In New York, I was broke and itinerant, but I made a community of friends like I'd never had before: my college roommate who wanted to be a novelist, the musicians and writers who frequented the concert venue where I worked, the journalists I met in graduate school. We all loved to talk and pick apart our lives, all shared a kind of unquenchable thirst, a restless kind of searching—for home, adventure, purpose, beauty. After finding kinship mostly in books as an adolescent, it was a rush to encounter it, finally, in real life. I had found *people like me*, I recall thinking.

Rachel was not *people like me*. She was a devoted Christian who tithed, went to Bible study, and had a weekly church group. I grew up without God, and spent most Sundays in my twenties either sleeping in or going to hungover breakfasts at greasy spoons. Rachel was silly where my New York friends were dry, affectionate where they were aloof. If we had met in different circumstances, we likely would not have become friends. But a few days after our husbands deployed, she invited me over for late night TV and wine. I jumped at the chance.

Miraculously, she had already set up her entire home, and her cream-colored carpet was so clean it showed fresh vacuum marks. We talked late into the night. She told me about how her husband, Dan, had rushed her into a courthouse wedding. She'd wanted something beautiful, traditional. "I had dreamed of my wedding my whole life," she said. I had never dreamed of a wedding of any kind, but I understood Rachel's disappointment. I had expected marriage to look different than this too. I thought my lifelong search for home had ended when I married Andrew, but now my home was on the other side of the world. I couldn't even call him. He had to trudge a half mile through snow to access a public phone, and if I missed it, we might not talk for another three days.

I was usually a guarded person, but that fell away almost immediately with Rachel. That night, I told her about how I felt as though Andrew, the only person who'd ever really loved me well, had abandoned me, though I knew he hadn't exactly left for milk never to return. Rachel confessed that she'd been reading the letters Dan wrote to her from boot camp to remind herself why on earth she'd upended her life for a man who was, so far, gone more than he was home.

After we'd finished a bottle of wine between us, I asked her, with some hesitancy, if she would be my emergency contact. Every spouse in the unit had to have someone command could call upon to help with life's quotidian details if their husband was injured or killed overseas.

She burst out laughing. "Are you kidding? Of course! You're already mine."

Back in my own house that night, I watched through the windows as Rachel turned out all her lights. Columbus was achingly quiet compared to New York; the silence was so loud it felt, almost, like a presence in the house. It was a comfort to know that Rachel was right across the street, and as I fell asleep, I thought of her laughter, how alive and shameless it was, how generous.

Over the next few months, Rachel haggled at estate sales to help me fill my house with furniture, cooked us Italian dinners, and even took us on big grocery shops so I didn't have to carry a week's worth of food from the handlebars of my bike. She gave her time and affection freely with no strings attached. It was becoming clear to me that this was her nature, but watching her, I understood that it was her reaction to loneliness. The lonelier I'd become in that first year of solitary marriage, the less I reached out to my scattered and busy community. Rachel's loneliness seemed, instead, to coax out of her this above-and-beyond neighborliness. This was an option, I realized, and by far a preferable one: to reach out rather than go inward. It's such an obvious truth, and yet, in what has been called the epidemic of loneliness we're living through, I think it's one we miss, or are too afraid to pursue—so much so that we often don't recognize another's invitation to connect. I began to read Rachel's way of moving through the world as a kind of instruction manual for my new life, bringing her takeout coffee whenever I grabbed some for myself, accompanying her on her dog walks, and roasting chicken and sweet potatoes for us on cold winter evenings.

My phone calls with Andrew that first deployment were often brief and strained. They were monitored, which made him so nervous as a new private that he'd hesitate to even tell me what he'd eaten for breakfast. In briefings and emails, the commanding officers would tell us spouses, "Your husbands can do what they do because of you." We got memos on how to be wives, on what to do and not do before, during, and after deployment. We were told: Don't let on where your husband is, what he does for a living. Don't ask when he'll be home, or why he seems so distant. Our primary assignment was silence. Rachel and I were both looking for a reason to stay in what felt like an impossible situation, and the reason we found was each other.

One drizzling morning, about a month into our husbands' absences, she called and asked if I wanted to go for a drive. There was a hint of mischief in her voice.

When she arrived at my door, she took her keys out of her back pocket and put them in my palm. Rachel had been threatening to take me on a driving lesson. "I love being your chauffeur, but you need to learn for yourself," she said gently.

We inched our way along the quiet streets of our neighborhood for a few minutes, the slowly moving windshield wipers creating a steady hum. She did most of the talking while I focused on the road, leaning over the steering wheel like an old lady even though there wasn't another car in sight. When we got to a stoplight, she mentioned a post she saw in the Facebook group for the battalion's Family Readiness Group (FRG), a collection of volunteer spouses that supported families in the unit with meal trains after mass casualties, diapers and baby blankets after births, and holiday meals during deployments. We were encouraged to introduce ourselves in this virtual space, but I hadn't yet. The page felt like a portal to a world I didn't really belong to yet, in part because it seemed geared toward families, so I lurked on the periphery, clicking through birth announcements and pictures of children in pumpkin patches. The prayer requests made me feel especially on the outside. *I need your prayers, warriors*, someone would post when their toddler was getting tubes in his ears or the family dog needed to go to the vet.

"I never know what to say on those things," I said. The light turned green, and I made a left to avoid the main streets.

"You don't have to believe in God to pray," she replied.

Maybe she was right. When I was a kid, I had prayed to a God I was pretty sure I didn't believe in: *Please let my mother come home safely, please make my parents stop fighting, please let my home calm the hell down.* Lately, lying in bed and watching the shadows fall across the wall as I had when I was small, I started praying again, out of desperation: *Please, keep Andrew safe. Bring him home to me.*

"And religious spaces can be for everyone," Rachel continued. "I'm meeting a lot of people at my church. Maybe you could find something church-like?"

I wasn't sure what that would be. Maybe a Unitarian Church? As a child, I had gone to one with a friend's family and still fondly remembered the scent of the warm apple cider we drank at the end of the service. The idea of walking into a room full of strangers unnerved me, though.

We reached a busy intersection.

"Now it's time to drive in some actual traffic. Turn right here."

"Like, where the people are?" I asked, feeling my chest tighten. Driving the empty neighborhood streets had been easy. Negotiating space and time with other drivers sounded downright terrifying.

"Yes, the people," she said, laughing.

"The people scare me."

After that, we referred to "the people" with fear in our voices whenever I was hesitant to do anything social—join her at a spouse retreat, go to a barbecue at her church, show up for an FRG event. But if Rachel asked me to accompany her, I almost always said yes.

When Rachel and her husband moved a mile away a little more than a year after that first deployment, it felt surprisingly far. She was pregnant with a baby girl, and they decided it was time to buy a house with a VA loan. It was disorienting to no longer her see her brewing coffee in her kitchen window in the mornings or rolling out her trash cans as the sun rose. I helped her set up the nursery and pick paint colors, but I hadn't realized how much her reliable presence had moored me, kept me from drifting like I had that year alone in New York.

Rachel had become busy with her church leadership team and baby story times, and I was busier too, teaching poetry workshops at an after-school program and running an editing business. Our lives had grown and expanded, much like my life and those of my New York friends during our twenties. I had become the treasurer for Andrew's company's FRG and found among the women I met in this group the most impressive community builders I'd ever seen. This was a skill I'd never truly valued or even taken the time to name. When one woman lost her pregnancy at six months during her husband's deployment, the FRG banded together to bring her meals. When a soldier rear-ended me at a yield sign, breaking my neck, they did the same for me after my spinal surgery. As much as I'd always wanted to belong, I had never been a joiner; I didn't see a place where I fit. But, in Georgia, I decided fitting didn't really matter. Showing up did.

New friendships grew out of the FRG for me: Hailey was a sarcastic, smart mom of two who loved to gather everyone at her house for barbecues, and Maggie was a journalist-turned-stay-at-home-mom with lightning-quick wit. I watched Hailey's kids from time to time and came to their school events as her plus-one. She picked me up when I locked myself out of my car after a morning hike, hauled a Christmas tree to my house after I had rotator cuff surgery, and invited me over for dinner on many lonely evenings. As the first sergeant's wife, Maggie was my font of wisdom and information, a guide who helped me make sense of my new world.

But there remained something special about my bond with Rachel: we had come up in our own ranks together. And so I was the person who accompanied her to every OB appointment while her husband was deployed. Later, three years into our time in Georgia, when I was thirteen weeks pregnant and our husbands were once again overseas, she was the one I texted when I felt like I was beginning to lose my mind. I always worried about Andrew's safety, but that deployment was different. I was utterly captive to what Google told me was perinatal anxiety, spending every night watching through the window for the headlights of a notification officer coming to inform me that my husband was dead.

Rachel didn't miss a beat. *Come over now, in your pajamas*, she texted back.

She led me to her guest room and told me to spend the night. I slept more deeply than I had in weeks, waking the next morning to her toddler tapping on my door, the room flooded with late morning light. Pretty soon, I was spending so many nights at Rachel's house that my Maps app began to register it as home. She understood, before I even did, that I needed something more than friendship, at least in the way we think of friendship in our society.

I needed that reliable, sturdy feeling of home I'd spent my whole life longing for, and she gave it to me, freely and without condition.

For the next five months I spent nearly every night at Rachel's brick colonial. She slow cooked us brisket, filling the house with the scent of rosemary, and I did the dishes. I babysat her toddler at her church nursery while she sang with the choir. She was the first person to feel my baby's kicks. After calls about casualties overseas, we'd reconvene in Rachel's den wordlessly. On the phone with my husband, I was my best, most buoyant self, protecting him, I thought, from the burden of worrying about me. Then I'd hang up, turn to Rachel, and tell her how afraid I was: of losing my husband, the baby, myself.

We knew our time together was temporary. And yet, I lived every day of that time with the sensation that she would always be there. That was what home felt like, I began to understand—the closest, most secure attachment, something I hadn't found among those friends in New York, or even in my own marriage. Because in my marriage, as in Rachel's, we sacrificed something greater than birthdays and anniversaries and Christmas mornings. It's something profoundly commonplace but sacred in family life: an assurance, however unfounded, that tomorrow will look like today. Maybe that was what I'd always been searching for, in an unpredictable and uncertain world. We knew that when our husbands got back, I'd return to my house, and a few months later, Andrew and I would relocate to Washington state. Rachel's own husband was thinking of getting out of the army. But for a time, we had a feeling of forever in each other.

Even in the brief moments the spotlight shines in our direction as military spouses, it's so rare that we are actually seen. Maybe that's why we are such incredible architects of community. What we build is not quite the same as what the soldiers have—an unquestioning loyalty, a knowledge that they would die for one another. Their bond is about their individual relationships, but it's also about belonging to an institution, to history. It is highly visible, celebrated at ceremonies and unit balls. Ours grows in the shadows, out of the very human desire to be seen. Yes, we need each other in a practical sense. But it's only together that we get to share the secret of our lives: not just the logistics of where our husbands might be or when they'll arrive home, but the world we create and inhabit together in their absence.

Q&A *with* MARY ANNE ADAMS

The Biggers House is a testament to what can be achieved when a community comes together to support its most vulnerable. It's about allowing our Black lesbian elders to age with dignity and community support, affirming that they are not alone.

When Mary Anne Adams was twelve years old, she had the opportunity to learn about Black literature and history while being surrounded by civil rights activists in Oxford, Mississippi. At the Black House, a hub for education and activism next door to Mary Anne's school, she spent afternoons listening to NAACP members, lawyers, and social workers as they organized, and soon became a volunteer. This was the start of her five decades of work on behalf of communities as a social worker, public health researcher, and community organizer.

For Mary Anne, now in her seventies, "The only reason we're on this planet is to help each other."

In 2011, Mary Anne founded ZAMI NOBLA: National Organization of Black Lesbians on Aging. ZAMI NOBLA works to combat the invisibility of Black lesbians over the age of forty by centering service, advocacy, and community action research; increasing opportunities for networking and social support; and exploring the healthcare needs of this group. The organization also aids in finding—and is working toward providing—housing for Black lesbian elders.

In conversations with peers, Mary Anne has noticed a conflict for some Black lesbian elders who talk about wanting to live in community, but who value their hard-won economic independence from the crowded homes they grew up in. As the second oldest of ten children, she intimately understands this contradiction. While Mary Anne doesn't have all the answers around how the social needs of Black lesbian elders might be addressed through communal living, she is interested in figuring it out, in part by embarking on a tiny house project with ZAMI NOBLA. Mary Anne and I discussed her efforts to create community for Black lesbian elders and the barriers to achieving safe, affordable, and supportive housing for all elders.

Why did you start ZAMI NOBLA and how have your personal experiences inspired what you've done with the organization?

I founded ZAMI NOBLA because I was fifty-seven years old and saw that older lesbians were disappearing from organizations and community-based activities in metro Atlanta. There seemed to be nowhere for them to go and nothing for them to gather around. As a community social worker and public health researcher, I knew that social isolation often leads to loneliness, depression, and other mental and physical health challenges. So, ZAMI NOBLA emerged out of a fierce determination to bring together and amplify the voices of Black lesbians by creating an organization where our specific struggles and triumphs are not just an afterthought but the focal point.

In building this organization, I was also looking to honor a neighbor I had nearly fifty years ago, Miss Savannah, who has been riding on my shoulder, whispering in my ear, and reminding me to remember the elders. I was nine years old, living in Freedmantown—a small community in Oxford, Mississippi, which newly freed Black people moved to and developed after the Civil War—when I met Miss Savannah. Despite wielding a shotgun at any child who walked across her lawn, she took a liking to me, a painfully shy bookworm. Even at a young age, I noticed she was socially isolated with three grown children who rarely visited. Most days, we were each other's only friend. Miss Savannah taught me how to knead dough and bake biscuits, regaled me with stories of her childhood, and was the first human who loved me unconditionally. She taught me about the civil rights movement, which really ignited a fire in me. She is a big part of the reason that I've found ways to leave a positive footprint in this world, and I always honor her life as an elder through my work.

What is the significance of ZAMI NOBLA being a specifically all-Black organization?

ZAMI NOBLA provides a safe space for Black lesbians to discuss and share our experiences without fear of racism or misunderstanding from those outside our racial or cultural background. In many spaces, Black lesbians are rendered invisible and often silenced, which can be especially true in mainstream LGBTQ+ spaces that do not always adequately address racial issues. ZAMI NOBLA is committed to building power and empowering our members by focusing on health inequities, economic challenges, and social oppression that disproportionately affect us.

Research on the unique experiences of Black lesbians, especially the impacts of racialized ageism, is scant. ZAMI NOBLA is the only national organization led by Black lesbian feminists fully dedicated to undertaking this research. We also advocate for specific policy changes and social recognition that speak to the needs of Black lesbians, such as mandatory cultural competence training for healthcare providers, social service workers, and policymakers; strengthening antidiscrimination laws in healthcare, employment, and housing that explicitly include sexual orientation, gender identity, and racial identity as protected categories; and policy reforms that consider nontraditional family structures and caregiving configurations common within the LGBTQ+ communities, which can affect retirement benefits and Social Security. By focusing exclusively on Black lesbians, ZAMI NOBLA helps to build a strong sense of community and solidarity among our members. This is affirming in a world where we often feel isolated or sidelined in both the broader Black and LGBTQ+ communities.

Tell me more about what feels most urgent to you when thinking about creating community.

Since we focus on supporting an older demographic, it's really important for us to close the digital gap. As we try to build community, we often run into a big hurdle when it comes to communication. Many of our older members, who aren't as comfortable with technology, struggle because they don't have reliable internet, the latest devices, or easy-to-use platforms. This makes it tough for us to keep everyone connected and informed. It's even harder for members who live on their own or live in rural parts of the country. Because ZAMI NOBLA operates nationwide and mostly online, the challenges don't stop there. Some of our members aren't familiar with how to use the internet, and others just can't afford it. This really limits our ability to offer continuous help and to keep our educational and support services—which focus on everything from financial literacy and estate planning to sexual and mental health—running smoothly, which are key to keeping everyone connected and trying to ensure that our members are well. It's crucial for us to find ways to bridge this digital divide so we can stay united and support each other effectively, no matter where we are.

What is the Biggers House? How does it provide support to Black lesbian elders surrounding housing and how has it helped ZAMI NOBLA foster community?

Back in 2014, we conducted focus groups here in Atlanta with one hundred Black lesbians whose ages spanned from forty-one to ninety-one years old.[1] One clear message emerged: housing was a major concern for them. Despite being well-educated—eighty-four had some college education or more—many were unemployed or stuck in under-the-table jobs, often due to discrimination surrounding their openness about their sexuality and their desire to live authentically. Unfortunately, this often meant missing out on crucial benefits like Social Security and retirement plans, leaving them vulnerable as they aged.

Recognizing this need, Dr. Edith Biggers, a public health physician and a board member of ZAMI NOBLA, offered the organization her childhood home in 2018. The catch was we had to fix it up. Though we were short on cash and repair skills, we were driven by a vision: to transform this seventy-five-year-old house into a safe, affordable sanctuary for Black lesbian elders. We envisioned the Biggers House for Black Lesbian Elders as a home that would support two elderly women on fixed incomes. We rallied the community for help, partnering with local organizations like Atlanta Pride, the Atlanta Fire Rescue Department, and Georgia State University's School of Social Work. Our fundraising efforts went viral, with donations pouring in from across the country. After four years of relentless effort, we welcomed our first resident.

The Biggers House is also a community hub, boasting five community gardens that not only provide fresh produce but also a place for people to connect. We've hosted three annual planting events, drawing volunteers of diverse ages, races, and backgrounds. These gatherings aren't just about gardening. They're about fostering unity and togetherness, and ensuring everyone has access to what they need. The Biggers House is a testament to what can be achieved when a community comes together to support its most vulnerable. It's about allowing our Black lesbian elders to age with dignity and community support, affirming that they are not alone.

Can you tell me about your plans to build tiny houses in the backyard of the Biggers House and what you hope this will accomplish?

ZAMI NOBLA recently began an environmentally sustainable project for the Biggers House by adopting an eco-friendly landscape design. This innovative design features the addition of three tiny houses within the property. The primary goal of constructing these tiny houses is to enhance housing affordability and accessibility for up to six Black lesbian elders, offering them a dignified and communal living environment. This initiative not only aims to provide a safe and affordable housing solution but also to foster a sense of community and belonging.

What kinds of changes in the ways we think about communal living do you hope to see in the next ten years?

I would love to see more public discussions around communal living. Changes in housing policies and financial models that support communal living are essential. This includes creating more flexible zoning laws, cooperative housing ownership models, and financial subsidies that make communal living accessible to more people. I would like to see sustainable practices, such as shared resources, eco-friendly building materials, and communal gardens that promote self-sufficiency and reduce ecological footprints. I hope to see communities that integrate various support systems for healthcare, elder care, and childcare. By pooling resources and responsibilities, residents can ensure that everyone, especially the most vulnerable like the elderly and children, is cared for adequately. Utilizing technology to enhance living conditions while ensuring privacy and security could be revolutionary. Smart home technologies can manage resource use more efficiently and improve overall quality of life, making communal living more comfortable and convenient.

You've advised other organizations on aging, housing, and creating community. What can we as individuals—and our country as a whole—do better with when it comes to addressing aging?

It's crucial to understand that elders are diverse, and it's time that our differences are recognized and respected. This is especially true for LGBTQ elders, who often face unique challenges and deserve to live without oppression due to our distinct needs. In 2019, ZAMI NOBLA played a key role in establishing the Metro Atlanta Lesbian and Trans Housing Alliance. This alliance spans races and generations and is led by dedicated lesbian and trans individuals. Our main goal is to tackle the specific housing issues that plague the LGBTQ community, with a special focus on elders. Our organization knows all too well that lesbian and transgender individuals are disproportionately affected by housing insecurity and homelessness. That's why we're committed to advocating for solutions that address these unique challenges. Mainstream housing programs often overlook our community, so our united, strong force works tirelessly to amplify our voices and leverage our resources to drive real change. We're not just fighting for visibility. We're here to ensure that all elders in our community have access to safe, affordable, and supportive housing. A place where dignity and respect are a given, allowing us to truly thrive.

DRAG IN THIS HOUSE

Jake Montano aka Imelda Glucose

> *Having a collective identity that is built around expressing, reclaiming, and reinventing queerness has a healing factor in a world that so readily shames or erases us.*

I was nine years old the first time I applied makeup to my face. It was rouge that my older sister, who was barely a teen, had somehow gotten ahold of. I was used to hanging out together in her room, secretly getting lost in the dreamy eyes of celebrities ripped from pages of *Teen Vogue* she had emblazoned on her walls. But, on this day, she wasn't home and I'd been lured into her room by a new gold-foiled stick of makeup sitting on her dresser. Looking in the mirror, I applied the lipstick with amateur enthusiasm while Mandy Moore's "Candy" played from a compact disc. Mouthing the lyrics, I pranced and swayed, revealing the suppleness of my left shoulder as I pulled the collar of my crewneck to the side—*maganda.* I imagined myself as a Filipina damsel, like I'd seen in telenovelas: beautiful, mysterious, but captive. This was a special episode in the programming of my preadolescent life. And it was a short one, because without even being seen or reprimanded, I knew the pigment had to come off before I left the room. I'd watched more than enough TV to understand what happened to boys who wore girls' things. I savagely rubbed the makeup off and joined my family downstairs.

Now, I tend to think about things other than the terror of getting caught. I consider whether I should redraw the liner to make my lips comically fuller, or leave them thinner for earnestness if I'm going to perform an Adele or Tracy Chapman banger. Sometimes I fantasize about what it would be like to get "into face," which is what we drag artists call getting ready, with my sister, who is now a mom and barely has time to do her own makeup, or with my mom, who has never really worn any. As I trace the contours of my lips with gloss or glitter, I picture how it will catch the light better on stage later.

Applying the finishing touches of blush and setting spray to keep everything in place for as long as possible, I mull over logistical details: how to get from my apartment to the door of the car. How I should greet the driver with my va-va-voom hair and extravagant costume so he doesn't drive off immediately. What route we're taking and where I'm getting dropped off. And most importantly, what blunt object to bring for self-defense should the need arise. I am in my tenth year as drag queen Imelda Glucose, a disco diva with a penchant for props and body contour dresses, and I've come to learn a few things about what the world thinks of people like me.

Drag is enjoying a moment in the spotlight, helped in no small part by pop culture phenomena like *RuPaul's Drag Race*, Tyler Perry's Medea films, and Chappell Roan. It isn't uncommon nowadays to find it on big marquees or as a passing reference during watercooler conversations. Although drag has always been around in some form or another, it has reached a zenith in its visibility and snackability, especially among non-queer audiences. And yet, despite all this, the number of hate crimes against queer people has climbed in recent years. We've seen the proliferation of hundreds upon hundreds of anti-trans and anti-drag bills, some from cities once known to be meccas of refuge for queer people.[1] *Psychology Today* recently reported that nearly half of queer-identified teens are estranged from at least one member of their families, and that queer-identified adults are more than twice as likely to choose distance from their immediate families due to worries about or lived experiences of rejection.[2] Drag might be increasingly prolific in the pop culture vernacular, but violence still persists for many of us.

Back in the 1970s, in response to this violence and shame, mass migrations of queer and trans people fled the suburbs and rural parts of America for major cities like New York, Chicago, or Philadelphia where they went on to form social groups of their own.[3] First motivated by affinity or attraction, the newfound proximity to other queer folks also produced conditions for different varieties of relationships, both platonic and romantic. These chosen families acted as support systems for elders to share wisdoms and practical knowledge around expression, health, and sex with younger queers, and were fertile grounds for creativity and collaboration. They came to be known as "houses," a cheeky reference to and subversion of the Western notion of the nuclear family, and have gone on to become the foundation of how drag and trans identity manifest today. Houses have their own mothers and fathers, with no commitment to norms of gender. These roles are instead built around dynamics of care or mentorship, especially for trans and non-binary people traversing the vastness of their own inner worlds of identity alongside an outer world of legal documentation, gender-affirming procedures, and social mores.[4]

My drag family members, Pei Pei Ma'Bilz, Panda Dulce, Saigon Dion, and April Mei Joon left my apartment hours ago, although scents of bacon and hair spray still waft through my kitchen. We gather like this, over food, wigs, and stories, at least once every couple of months. During today's brunch, we reviewed our slate of recent and approaching gigs, including our fifteenth-year anniversary show, and enjoyed catching up on each other's personal lives. We also devised strategies for me to compete in an upcoming pageant called Runway (presented by the GLBTQIA+ Asian-Pacific Alliance), which is one of the largest drag events in our community. We daydreamed and schemed: What concepts make sense for the fantasy talent showcase? Who can be called upon to help style wigs? Who knows how to sew? What other houses are competing?

Our house, called the Rice Rockettes, is headed by our matriarch, Estée Longah, who cofounded the troupe in 2009. Since I asked Estée to be my coach and handler backstage on the day of the pageant, she has lingered at my apartment to study sketches of dresses and storyboards I've made. We are piecing together our strategy and running through hard-hitting questions we expect I'll be asked during the interview portion of the show, while she revisits the early days of our drag family.

Houses came about at a time when "queer people were denied by their families and kicked out of their homes," Estée tells me. The Rice Rockettes, among the oldest all-Asian and Pacific Islander (AAPI) drag troupes in America, formed to unite the AAPI drag community in the Bay Area. According to Estée, "There weren't very many Asian drag queens in any place around the Bay that you could find. You could count them all on one hand."

Before 2009, drag lacked most of its name recognition outside of people like RuPaul, Divine, or Mrs. Doubtfire. Even in San Francisco, which features one of the oldest Chinatowns in the world and one of the most diverse populations of the Asian diaspora, it was uncommon to encounter queer and AAPI people in public places.

Across queer nightlife in the city, one of the few enclaves of Asianness could be found at the now-closed N'Touch Bar on Polk Street, where you might have run into Tita Aida ("Auntie AIDS" in Tagalog). A health educator, organizer, and activist, she ran HIV/AIDS services and community programs for queer and trans locals at the Asian & Pacific Islander Wellness Center, now the San Francisco Community Health Center, and was the host of a weekly drag show at N'Touch that incorporated community outreach. The show was often headlined by the Rice Girls, a CDC-funded, Tita Aida-led collective of queer and trans health educators who donned drag and danced as they offered strategies for better and safer sex, then performed renditions of songs by the Spice Girls. Estée was a newer drag queen at the time, and Tita Aida took her under her wing as performer and organizer, becoming her drag mother. When CDC funding ended for the Rice Girls, Estée applied her experience to forming the Rice Rockettes.

This group has been a family to me since I moved to the city from Orange County, leaving behind a past of severe closetedness. They guided and encouraged me as I learned to embody my queerness and flamboyance, and rediscovered my Filipinoness, in the streets of a new city. Through them, I conjured Imelda Glucose. Ever since my debut in drag, Estée has been both a mentor and friend—and I'm one of many who have benefited from her tutelage and experience in community health, queerness, and drag pageants.

Drag pageants first took place in the 1960s, but they have roots and inspiration in beauty pageants dating as far back as the mid-1800s. They don't play a major role in every drag queen's life, but they are major events for everyone involved in them. Highly competitive, even cutthroat, pageants have multiple categories—talent, formal wear, interview—and contestants vying to win them and other distinctions like "Miss Congeniality." They're flamboyant, glamorous, and sometimes campy events of pomp and circumstance that can be satirical and exultant of identity politics in the same stride. In Black and brown cities across the South and East Coast, more culturally rooted variations, called balls, began to form. As balls became entrenched in neighborhoods that also experienced racialized disinvestment and persistent housing crises, older competitors extended creative mentorship to younger competitors, as well as rooms in their homes, establishing the house system and the modern ballroom scene. With visions of something more, these intergenerational homes became a creative nucleus, conjuring new forms of queer expression from voguing (a stylized and surrealist modern house dance) to reading (a form of playful and witty insult comedy) to contouring (using makeup to enhance light and shade on the face). Such innovations have further distinguished ballroom from pageants and influenced non-queer mainstream culture globally.

The Rice Rockettes exist more in the world of pageants, nightlife, and cultural community than in balls. Our group of a dozen or so active Rockettes—and just as many retired members spanning six generations—is a drag troupe, and for many of us, our chosen family. The name Rice Rockettes is a familial catchall for the many lineages that make up our group. Like other families, individual Rockettes have defined dynamics that connect us to one another: drag mothers and fathers, daughters, aunties, and big sisters. Mothers choose their daughters and act as mentors, friends, or parental stand-ins as new members acclimate. Some retired Rockettes continue to play vital roles, providing safety, wayfinding, and tech support for events. Many other Rockettes who have retired from drag and regular participation still join us as audience members, collaborators, and close friends, turning gatherings into mini reunions.

Chosen family like I've developed within the Rice Rockettes plays a critical role in addressing and remedying experiences of homophobia or microaggressions. As brunch turns into happy hour in my apartment, Estée and I sip mimosas, and she recounts times when the Rice Rockettes were mocked and called "he-shes" as they walked down the famously gay Castro Street. But she says, overall, she has felt safe—and when members of her community are sometimes targeted for violence, the Rice Rockettes are always there for each other. I was lucky to have them earlier this year.

June, otherwise known as Pride Month, is a busy season of gigs and gatherings for drag artists. It is also when the veil between genders thins to its finest for many of us, who daywalk with leftover eyeliner from the previous night's gig as we balance tight turnarounds between corporate parties, club events, parades, and our nine-to-five jobs. In celebration of the season, I was wearing flashy jewelry to my job running after school programs at a local museum and piled my long hair into a loose bun as an ode to my gender-bending. This caught the attention of two homophobes garbed in oversize cargo pants at the bus stop near my house. Over and over, they called me "faggot" as they backed me into a concrete wall. They closed in on me, but almost as quickly as the incident started, it ended when they noticed the presence of nearby safety patrol officers, who watched but never intervened. My attackers fled the scene after a final spew of epithets and left me silenced, in tears.

The experience almost claimed my life in the weeks after. I spent most of my time in bed as the memory of my assailants' faces and vitriolic words revisited me against my will. I felt little consolation from my birth family, who misunderstood the incident and my experience, chalking it up to a lack of situational awareness on my part and as *just another one of those things that happens in the world we live in*. It was a reminder text from Estée and my drag auntie Chi Chi, another cofounder of the Rice Rockettes, that disrupted the loop I had gotten lost in. The message sent the logistics for a rehearsal we had agreed to weeks before, in preparation for a theatrical production around queer narratives we were set to do the following weekend. Estée and Chi Chi had offered me the space to step back and focus on my recovery, but I felt it would be detrimental to the production if our piece, which was the only vignette that involved drag, did not come to fruition.

It was soothing to be in the presence of close friends and healthy to occupy a headspace outside of my trauma. The piece we were featured in had Estée cast as my mother, in drag, and me, out of drag, playing the semi-autobiographical role of the playwright as he navigated the awkwardness and toil of coming out to her as HIV-positive. It allowed each of us to relay and explore the layers of our own relationships with biological families and to reframe them through the dramatization. I often cried after rehearsals, unsure of what was inspiring the tears, between the piece and flashbacks of my recent hardships. It felt safe and therapeutic to bring my personal inflections to the story, which our director Chi Chi encouraged. When we debuted the following weekend, many of the Rockettes attended, furthering the feeling of being supported by a family who saw not only my pain but also me and my art.

Part of the magic of a drag house, or a chosen family, is the way they offer us the opportunity to bring vital aspects of our identities and daily lives—for us, our queerness—out of invisibility or otherness to the surface, conjuring celebration and activity around them. They may lack definition by blood or marriage, but chosen families make up for it with emotional safety and shared values.[5] Queerness itself evokes infinity, and having a collective identity that is built around expressing, reclaiming, and reinventing it has a healing factor in a world that so readily shames or erases us.

Across years and moments of hangouts and gigs, every Rockette has opened up about the dynamics of our birth families. About the silence that can fall between a mother and child after coming out. About the holiday gatherings that trigger deep-seated anguish or alienation. About the years of work and repair that get you to another side with more acceptance and understanding. About the familiar silence that shows up again when you come out a second time as a drag queen, with all of society's mudslinging projected on to you. While revisiting some of these memories, I disclose to Estée how disappointed I feel that my family does not seem interested in attending the pageant, or in anything I do related to my longtime work and life as a drag queen and community organizer.

Estée holds my hand firmly: "Oh honey, we should be so lucky to have birth families who care to know us like that." A hard truth in the form of a bitter pill, and the only salve is knowing that Estée understands what this feeling is like. "I don't have a relationship with my family," she reminds me. "The Rice Rockettes are more my family than my actual relatives are anymore."

I point out a cloak I sketched in my notebook and ask Estée which Rockette she thinks could help me construct an absurd but potentially stunning garment for one of the pageant looks I'm planning—a monarch caterpillar that hearkens back to the Victorian style of a 1920s socialite. Without hesitation, she quips, "Your mother."

When the Rice Rockettes met me, I was out of the closet but yet to relish my authenticity and flamboyance. Discovering them and the way they merged their identities with their art was transformational, and instantly, I wanted to try it for myself. When I joined my drag family, I chose the name Imelda Glucose as a way to reconnect with my Filipino heritage and effeminate nature, and as a personal reclamation after years of feeling diminished because of these traits.

On the day of the pageant, performers are called backstage and Estée grabs my hands for a final calming circle between the two of us. Calming circles are a Rice Rockettes ritual before every performance, and I revel in this moment of solace. We take deep breaths, and she reminds me to find my joy and my voice out on the stage. I couldn't have grown in my expression and identity without Imelda, and Imelda wouldn't be the queen she is without family like Estée, or other Rice Rockettes members like Doncha, Vermicelli, and Kristi. As the house lights go down and music floods the room, I channel each of them and the myriad ways they've inspired, taught, comforted, and loved me.

This is my tenth year as Imelda Glucose, and I feel so much more ready to take on the world than when I began. And no matter what happens, I know I'll be okay: I'm a Rice Rockette.

Q&A *with* ADAM MEYER

It felt like a remarkable decline in communal eating, and I tried to bridge that for myself and others when I began my dinner parties.

Adam Meyer has a spreadsheet in which he tracks the names of people who have attended the weekly and monthly dinner parties he has hosted over the last two years. Some of these people grew up in Jackson Hole, Wyoming, while others moved to the area in adulthood, as Adam did. Some were friends of friends, and even friends of friends of friends, just passing through. There are over 120 names on Adam's spreadsheet, and he is thrilled to have shared a meal with every single one.

Growing up in southern Maine with his parents and sister, Adam, now in his twenties, learned about community from the regular dinner gatherings his parents held. After dinner, when everyone at the kids' table would go off to play, he preferred to join the discussion at the adults' table. "I've always been an enthusiast of the talking part of dinner parties," he says.

Communication and intentionality are at the core of Adam's dinner party efforts, which he began during his junior year at Tufts University. Those gatherings were a little more casual; these days, he invites attendees individually over text and keeps track of who joined, who declined, and most importantly, who never responded. His policy: If you don't respond to an invite, you won't be asked to the dinner party immediately following. "I still love you, but ghosting is not acceptable," he explains.

He's seen a major decline in the practice as a result. Recently, Adam threw his biggest dinner party yet with forty-four people between their early twenties and late thirties—and he expects that number to keep growing. Adam and I talked about the intricacies of building community through recurring dinner gatherings and what draws Gen Z to seek shared spaces.

What drove you to start hosting dinner parties as a college student, which is already a community-oriented experience? Can you tell me how those gatherings worked?

A college dining hall is the pinnacle of community. At Tufts, everyone is required to get an unlimited meal plan your first two years, but during your junior and senior years, you're not, so there's this dramatic drop off in on-campus dining participation. In these later years, you might overlap with your housemates for lunch, you might overlap for dinner, but you might have totally different schedules. It felt like this remarkable decline in communal eating, and I tried to bridge that for myself and others when I began my dinner parties in my final two years of college.

It started with just the eight of us living in our house. I was catering during weekends back in Maine, and I would bring home all these lobster rolls and other delicious treats that we'd eat in our backyard. Then I started inviting friends over and it got to the point where we had to figure out how many people we could have in our common room each week without the floor sagging into the apartment below. We had a small, grassy backyard, but next to it was a dilapidated pool with a fence around it. I always said we'd fill in the pool, put twinkle lights over the top of it, and have amazing dinner parties out in the backyard. Unfortunately, the pandemic disrupted this plan. During my senior spring, everything shut down.

When and where did you resume hosting and how did you get the word out? Did you have new goals pertaining to starting this up again post-college?

I moved to Jackson Hole two years ago, in 2022, to work as a cross-country ski coach, and I was living in employee housing with two other ski coaches. Both of my housemates had lived here and already had friends, and I just said, "Hey, I would love to meet your friends. Let me cook everybody dinner." So that's how my dinner parties have restarted, as a way to get to know my housemates' friends, and now it's a way for me to get to know my friends' friends, and my friends' friends' friends. I'm really grateful that we've got this going on here.

I think the goal is the same: meeting cool people, fostering community, breaking bread, and occasionally showing off my chef skills. For the first year and a half, it was me cooking the main course, and guests bringing appetizers. This summer, it's morphed from a weekly affair into a monthly potluck, and rather than just hosting at my house, I've tried to have it in a few different locations. I have some friends who live up in Grand Teton National Park who have cohosted. We've dined on the banks of the Snake River. The idea is that once we get into winter, it'll go back to being a weekly thing at my house as the days grow shorter and it feels like there's a greater need for community.

Do the same people tend to come back again and again? Do you often have new people show up?

People do come back and it's awesome. But in the winter, because I'm cooking the main course and I don't want to cook for forty people every single week, sometimes I might bump a loyalist from the invite list to allow someone new or someone who usually can't come to experience the magic of this community and get to know all these people. Folks who get bumped from the list are normally understanding of my desire to share the magic.

Also, plus-ones are strongly encouraged. My logic behind that is I know you, but I don't know all of your friends, and I'm sure your friends would love to meet my friends, and I'd love to have this mixing so that it's not the same people every week. I think of myself jokingly, but not totally jokingly, as the mayor of Jackson Hole. Not that many people live year-round in Jackson, and I feel like whenever I walk around town, I see people who've been to my dinner parties.

How do you determine your menu?

Sometimes it's seasonal, sometimes it's just fun, sometimes I take requests. I also have a theme and dress code that is typically accompanied by a Pinterest board I've created. In September, we did a fall mountain chic potluck and I made pasta salad. In August, it was neon brat and I made sweet potato curry. In July, it was animal print cowboy. In June, it was garden party, and in April, it was a fake wedding, all the way down to a fake bride, groom, ring bearer, and officiant. That was the only time I've ever been strict on a timeline. Folks, it's a wedding! I just accepted a position with the US ski team to be one of their chefs at a training camp in Colorado for a month, and I've been tossing around the idea of a future dinner party with a fancy dress code—a three-course plated affair using one of the dinner menus that I'll be serving to the ski team.

Overall, I think people want the opportunity to dress up, but many of those opportunities come with significant costs, like traveling cross-country for a wedding. But here, people can drive three minutes or ride their bicycle to my house. We have a fun night. We all look beautiful. We take group photos. We make it a night to remember.

What do you feel like attendees get out of the dinner party experience?

At least six potential romances have formed out of the dinner parties. I don't think any of them ended up being successful, but it was exciting that this person didn't know that person, and they hit it off because of my dinner party. I think we've had a few folks with potential job and housing leads come out of it. And then a bunch of friendships formed, especially across friend groups, between my swing dancing friends and my ski club friends. Watching the friendships blossom has been fun.

Gen Z has been called the "loneliest generation." You're also the first group of digital natives, your education was interrupted by the pandemic, and you're known for juggling jobs and side hustles in a time of financial insecurity and housing unaffordability. Do you personally connect to any of these cultural challenges?

I think I connect to all of them. Housing affordability is a big thing in Jackson. Of the one hundred-plus people who have been to my dinner parties, only one owns a home here, and he inherited it through the passing of a family member. We have one returning guest who is on the board of our local housing affordability nonprofit coalition. It's a popular topic at our dinner table.

In an ideal world, I'd love to be surrounded by my friends all living in one apartment building. I really did love that part of dorm life—walking by your neighbor's room, seeing their door open, and chatting for thirty minutes. I wouldn't say that I'm lonely. I would flip it and say I'm always looking for more opportunities to spend time with friends, whether it's informal like when I see my neighbor walking her dog and she stops by to say hi, or more planned, like calling people up to go on bike rides. I don't know how the other folks in my dinner party community feel, but I think that people are really excited when these gatherings happen, and they love being invited. That could be because they just love having something to look forward to and dress up for, or it could be loneliness.

What models for community and/or housing do you feel would best support your generation, and in your ideal world, what would this look like?

There's a lot of talk of communal living among my Jackson friend group, but with a particular focus on communes since there are all these massive tracts of land in neighboring valleys. I know multiple people who have looked into what would it take to buy a ten-acre plot of land and have twenty houses where we can all go visit each other easily, and where we would have land ownership, which is something that's not necessarily attainable for our generation in this location of millionaires and billionaires. I like the idea of proximity, but I dream of living in even greater proximity to the people I care about. My dream is that apartment-style living. Jackson has a lot of single-family housing, but after going to school in Boston, I'm a big believer in apartments for community building. You can leave notes and knock on doors super easily. But I would caveat with well-insulated walls. I'd like to be able to have very loud dinner parties and not annoy my neighbors.

How could leaning more into community address some of the challenges we face as a culture, and help us experience more understanding and joy?

I think we would be able to better understand what is affecting others. I want to ride my bicycle without being hit by a car, and I'm sure other people want that too. My female friends here in Wyoming want reproductive healthcare access not to be horrible, and I want that too. If we have a stronger community, then we can better understand the shared goals that we all have, or the shared needs, and then from there, work together to create solutions that suit everybody.

What advice do you have for people who want to throw these kinds of dinner parties but don't know where to start?

Start small. Invite your closest friends first and then begin asking them to bring plus-ones. Then, when you're really comfortable hosting, invite acquaintances. Soon you'll be the unofficial mayor of your town!

THE OPPOSITE OF LONELINESS

Sarah Thankam Mathews

What Bed-Stuy Strong gave me a renewed appreciation for is that "community" is nothing more or less than a group of people and that people are beautiful, damaged, powerful, tiresome, maddening, and most of the time, worth it anyway.

In the language of the meme: Within me were two clowns. One romanticized community, one romanticized isolation. In my twenties and early teens, I had spent an inordinate amount of time thinking about the seductive subtle dangers of a life organized exclusively around the couple form, the suburban-propertied form, the form of the traditional nuclear family. These all seemed to be a recipe for long-term loneliness, and to my young self, loneliness was a long desert I had achingly traversed and hoped never to set foot in again. People are the answer, I intoned to myself, again and again, as I traveled from the ages of twenty to twenty-eight.

Time confounds. So does real experience: the kind that leaves you calloused or scarified or in possession of smile lines or perhaps the real tell—respectful of the difficulty and complexity of doing anything. I look back now and I wonder, *Did that really happen, and how?*

Well, it did happen. Here is the shortest telling I can manage: I turned twenty-nine and as the COVID-19 pandemic began its long ravage of the United States, I started a mutual aid collective in Central Brooklyn. It was an endeavor that began with putting up flyers on traffic poles in my 165,000-person neighborhood of

Bedford-Stuyvesant, days before shelter-in-place policies were put into effect. The mutual aid collective was called Bed-Stuy Strong. It was needfully coordinated online, hosted on the messaging platform Slack. Mere hours after the first hundred flyers were put up, it began to explode with activity. At its most robust, Bed-Stuy Strong had over five thousand active members and working groups on everything from sourcing high-quality PPE for healthcare workers to leftist political education to support for neighbors who had recently been released from prison. Bed-Stuy Strong, during the first year and change of its COVID-era food security operation, raised over $1.2 million from regular people and redistributed it to over 28,000 people, through cash assistance and grocery delivery. People who did not live through that time in New York, and even some people who did, forget how steeped in death and loss and fear the city was. BSS, as members called our mutual aid network internally, became—for some modest number of people—a place of togetherness, comfort, cooperation, and dreaming, which is to say, a space of life in a time of death.

The network changed as years moved through it and as the emergency it was formed in response to transformed in nature. I stepped down from leadership to focus on other projects, including my burgeoning work as a novelist and writer. BSS is still active today, in a smaller and focused form, a bantam, determined collective of people that works to do what we did from the beginning: support and care for each other and try to make sure people's basic needs for survival are being met while making space to question why, in the richest nation in the world, these needs exist in the first place.

The more detailed *how* of it all is a trickier needle to thread.

What turned into Bed-Stuy Strong began as a spiral of anxiety and rage. In March 2020, I was in the process of surfacing from a profound, months-long depression, a diver rising slowly from black water toward the light. The depression had some circumstantial backing. I was making a poverty-line amount of money. I had left a stable career to try to be a writer while freelancing and doing gig work, and this endeavor had not been bearing fruit. I had been doing badly, but I was getting better. And I'd been reading international news coverage of an emergent coronavirus and reckoning with the real possibility that New York might be about fourteen days behind Italy, then under full lockdown.

I remembered my next-door neighbor who was not in great health and wondered if he would be okay. Two thoughts danced inelegantly around my brain. *Nobody may come to help us in time; we are all we've got. We need to quickly organize, online and geographically.*

After looking to see if what I wanted existed already, I mapped out different ideas, sketching them on a legal pad—a series of connected private Facebook groups, branching WhatsApp phone trees—feeling increasingly unsatisfied, and then it hit me. Setting up a neighborhood-based network on the messaging app Slack would work well, at least as a start, and we could set up a phone number for neighbors without reliable internet access. I built out the Slack infrastructure in about forty-five minutes, with lighthearted channels like #pictures_of_pets, as well as channels for people to share what they needed or wished to organize around. I made a quick how-to resource in case other people might want to do this for their own neighborhoods and dropped it on what was then called Twitter.

Staring at the empty Slack channel, I felt a wild throb of preemptive embarrassment. What if no one joined? What if people joined and then were awful to each other? I texted a close friend these fears, and he very kindly told me to stop being a chump. I ran out and put a note on my neighbor's door, asking him to call me if he needed anything. My partner and I printed twenty pages of flyers, cut them up into quarter sheets, and then walked around my neighborhood of Bed-Stuy, putting them up on street corners and bodega doors.

This was March 14, right around when most people began to voluntarily try to stay at home, exactly one week before the shelter-in-place order was announced in New York. The flyers had a join link that took people to the Slack. By the time I got home, sixteen new people were in the network. By the end of the day, sixty-five. Neighbors began introducing themselves, expressing gratitude and relief that this existed. Again and again, people wrote *Here are my cross streets, This is what I do, I want to help.* The next day, eighty people joined, the day after, a hundred fifty, and Bed-Stuy Strong was born.

The *we* of Bed-Stuy Strong is what electrified and astonished me. We: my neighbors, my fellow organizers, the eventual thousands of ordinary people who raised a hand and said, *I want to do something.* We made a phone number on day two. We had an organizing meeting on Zoom: day four. We made a bilingual flyer and thirty volunteers papered the neighborhood with it: day six. We set up a rudimentary system—a neighbor would leave a message on the hotline and a member would call them back, find out what they needed, and post it on Slack for other neighbors to respond to or offer to contribute money to. Most of the neighbors who were calling needed groceries—they were older or immunocompromised and couldn't leave the house or they had been laid off and had no funds. We began to receive thirty to fifty calls a day. We set up a community fund to buy those groceries, stitching together cash apps like Venmo and PayPal and Zelle to a personal bank account. That, I think, was day eleven. Some of our members who had tech backgrounds raised their hands to try to build a more sophisticated system so we could help more people and faster, given that hunger is a pretty immediate need. We put it in motion. By the end of the first two weeks, over a thousand people had joined. It was terrifying but exhilarating too.

A few months later, I wrote about our work, in large part to publicize the network to raise funds that could then be used to buy more people food and medicine:

> A few years ago I had determined to never again let the ineptitude and cruelty of the current political administration shock me. No, I did not expect much of the US to respond to the burgeoning pandemic humanely or well. To say the least. Mutual aid, that is, reciprocal intra-community help and support expressed in a spirit of solidarity, is the heart of Bed-Stuy Strong, which today is a multiracial network of three thousand people from all walks of life, from grocery store clerks to software engineers to artists. In our first nine weeks of existence, we have supported over five

thousand neighbors with a week of groceries delivered to their door, creating an estimated 100,000 meals. It's absolutely wild to me. It demonstrates the power of emergent networks and of organizing, and the reality that most people are hungry to be decent in an indecent time.

Many of these neighbors pay it forward in some way; some join Bed-Stuy Strong and volunteer to run other deliveries, some offer contributions to the community as they can. The network has had multiple other initiatives its members are working on, from getting people to complete the census (Bed-Stuy was undercounted by an estimated 49% in 2010) to providing masks to healthcare workers to helping coordinate supplies for our neighbors who don't have homes.

Besides solidarity, we articulated other guiding principles for our work together: accountability, resourcefulness, care, imaginative thinking, joy, and crucially, humility. We know other community organizations have been doing the work for a long time. We were, and are, a volunteer-run network of ordinary people, and thus have to own our finiteness. We were, and have to be, part of a great patchwork of efforts to take care of our communities during a calamitous global crisis that has reverberated along long-standing fault lines of structural racism, economic inequality, and healthcare disparities. We saw, and see, any worthwhile thing we accomplish as a small part of the long legacy of joined hands here in Central Brooklyn. This is, after all, where the Black Panther Party set up a free medical clinic, abolitionists worked to get enslaved people to freedom, and people who were marginalized by the state in a variety of ways have looked out for each other, and shown up for each other, for a very long time.[1]

All of this was true and sincere and also, in the interstices of my words, looking back from years later, I see the culture of the moment I was writing from: a stormy time of reckoning, awareness of structural and historical injustice, the George Floyd uprising, the specter of online callouts and cancellations, the massification (and co-optation) of mutual aid in a way where an increasing number of people understood it to mean "virtuously helping people less fortunate," and what would later dismissively get called wokeness. Bed-Stuy is a historically Black neighborhood with a rich tradition of self-determination. In the early 2020s, it was continuing to gentrify rapidly, aided by city policies and legislators uninterested in reining in real estate interests in any meaningful way. While BSS had Black members and lead organizers, they were never in the majority. White guilt and shame reverberated through the network, as they were reverberating through American society at large, producing effects both useful and exhausting. The anxieties and ambivalences and confused etiquette of the time showed up, again and again, in the work behind the scenes.

It is worth asserting that mutual aid is something deeper and more interesting than "helping people." Mutual aid is premised on the recognition that everything in our society lives and dies by resource allocation: the ordering of shelter and food and care and money. It is, as a principle, interested in the idea that we might cooperatively allocate resources by something other than the profit motive, with an eye to solidarity, to the survival and flourishing of all. Mutual aid is practiced *most easily* in homogeneous environments, as an in-community tool, or as a tactic of community recruitment. Churches and mosques, gay people and men, Native and Black and South Asian people, all have their histories with the practice. Even some white supremacist groups practiced mutual aid. The success and challenge of Bed-Stuy Strong was inextricably tied to its insistence that *everyone* had needs and *everyone* could help and that something quietly radical could take place once a group of people's help met their own needs when the state was failing.

As founder, as a melanated person who is not Black, and as someone who was then willing to spend an hour or two on the phone with a perfect stranger who was brand-new to the network and looking for a place to put their anger about larger injustices, I spent a lot of energy navigating some people's conflicts with each other, their ambivalence around a non-Black-led mutual aid network in a historically Black neighborhood that anyone could join, or their discomfort with BSS's universalist framing of mutual aid, where anyone who lived in the neighborhood could access the network's benefits. I'm not sorry for the time I spent, and I believe the work I put in to help members resolve their conflicts genuinely helped the collective have a lifespan of more than a few months. But these dynamics, and the grinding and unpaid work in general, took a toll on me. One of the more active BSS members sexually harassed me; I dealt with it privately and capably enough but began to feel a deepening impatience with the ways in which I saw people in the collective idealize and sanctify other members based on identity and sexuality. I began to have a Pavlovian reaction to the Slack notification sound, which went off multiple times an hour throughout the day and night. My reaction was a sensation of clammy dread, a surreptitious quickening of the heart. I would think, *Oh no, what now?*

We were trying to build structures of care at a massive scale during a pandemic, during a time when it was dangerous to gather in person, with a wide membership across every possible axis of difference. I suppose part of what I'm saying is that it was always going to be difficult, in ways that I did not fully appreciate at the time. I'm glad we put up the flyers anyway.

I have often felt weird speaking about Bed-Stuy Strong as an *I*, a single self. For years, I mostly managed not to, when I wrote emails asking for money, spoke with reporters looking to tell a trend story, or DMed people explaining that no we were not a nonprofit or a food pantry with 501(c)(3) status, we were a membership-based organization, and they were welcome to join. Using *we* seemed easier and more truthful. Because BSS was the work of literally thousands of people, and in particular, the collectively harnessed genius and rigor of about nine organizers whose decisions and work shaped what BSS became. Because I know that the story of the organization would probably look quite different, depending on who was doing the telling—Hanna or Jackson, the lead organizers of our warehouse operation, among much else, or one of the moms receiving grocery support while using her car to get food for other families, or one of the many people who signed up to "help out" and, after completing a shift or four, returned to their lives.

But this is a personal essay, not an oral history. I founded Bed-Stuy Strong in a time of desperation. Together we all made it what it was. For me, it was a multiauthored attempt during a desperate time at what historian Kristin Ross calls the commune form, at trying to begin to imagine the unit of the neighborhood itself as a communistic space.[2] I helped run it for two years and then sometime during my third year with the group, I stepped down from it, truthfully citing a lack of time. I left unsaid something more complicated: that I was exhausted and aching for a hundred reasons; that I wanted to be a writer who had enough peace to think; that I wanted to be small and ordinary and have no good answers and be cared for anyway. I was proud of what we did together, a pride all the fiercer for being shot through with mourning. The collective gifted me with some of my closest friendships. It gave me the deep joy of putting principles into applied practice with clever and humble and determined people and watching them *actually work*. It exhilarated me, it taxed me, it wounded me, and it changed my life.

In the years that have passed since Bed-Stuy Strong was a twinkle in an HP printer's eye, I have felt increasingly bemused by a growing cultural emphasis on community as some kind of unadulterated good in everyone's lives. The people who wax most poetic about community, often but not always, live its practice in the thinnest and most theoretical ways. What Bed-Stuy Strong gave me a renewed appreciation for is that "community" is nothing more or less than a group of people and that people are beautiful, damaged, powerful, tiresome, maddening, and, most of the time, worth it anyway. If you want your life to be convenient and easy, being in deep relationship and comradeship with other people, especially across differences of race and class, is not what I might recommend.

Still, many of us are motivated to seek something other than a pure and bland *ease*.

I don't know if people are the answer. But for me, they will always be the question. After everything, the profound, dizzying pleasure of togetherness is my lasting impression of the early years of Bed-Stuy Strong. I think of vigils and free people's markets and block parties in Herbert Von King Park organized by people including Sky Hollenbeck, Derek Smith, and Alyssa Dizon. I think of Hadass Wade, who came to BSS after years of waiting tables, who indefatigably managed over a million dollars in our community fund and personally disbursed and tracked more than thirty thousand individual Venmo transactions. I think of Hanna King and Jackson Fratesi masterminding a warehouse operation in Brownsville with the worker-owned cooperative Brooklyn Packers, which allowed us to feed thousands more people at scale. I think of Alex, Nia, George, Sam, Unis, Hannah, Ivonne, and so many others who labored to make something startling and moving in its enormity. I think of spreadsheets and pallet jacks and weepy voicemails from strangers who were able to put food on their families' tables in a time of social breakdown. I remember parties and dinners and cry-laughing on Zoom. I remember street cleanups and dancing in the sun. I remember always having a place to turn to when bad things happened: what a shocking, precious gift. I remember sitting deathly sick on my stoop and having Chris Xu, then a stranger, who became one of my closest friends, glide up on Rollerblades to drop off medicine, looking like they'd materialized straight out of a Sega Dreamcast. I remember some of the deepest joy I've ever known, some of the fiercest exhilaration, the truly bodily-felt knowledge that we were powerful because we were together. It was the opposite of loneliness, all of it, the struggle and the triumph alike. That's what I've kept in my life ever since; it's what I wish for everyone.

WEATHERING

Kristen Arnett

Because of my friends, I wake up and understand that regardless of what's on the horizon—wedding or hurricane—I can move through life knowing that I won't have to do any of it alone.

This was a year of hurricanes and weddings.

I mean, I live in Florida, so it's almost always storm season. From May through November, it's not unusual for the sky to crack open, shed thunder and lightning, pour down the kind of rain that wants to drown you. I was raised Southern Baptist, evangelical. I grew up on biblical stories that told us to believe the impossible. Noah's Ark doesn't seem that farfetched when you consider the fact that Florida is slowly sinking back into the sea. Nobody understands that climate change is real more than a Floridian who's endured multiple hurricanes in a single year.

How best to stay afloat?

I've been estranged from my biological family for close to ten years. A decade without my mother, my father. I don't have contact with my brother, my uncles, my aunts, my grandmother. I receive occasional texts from these people, which I do not answer. They sit unopened on my phone, letters unread. The reality of the situation is that these family members are attempting to contact a person who does not exist, a person who maybe never existed, outside of memories they Frankensteined together from long past birthdays and holidays. Who is this fictitious daughter, niece, sister, grandchild? She is not me, but she shares my face. My voice. This version of Kristen is the memory of a child who wasn't gay. Who hadn't yet communicated her opinions. Who hadn't opened her mouth and suddenly turned into a stranger. Who didn't make a fuss about her political beliefs. It's a version of myself who sat in a corner, quietly, and kept my lips zipped.

I'm without my biological family, but I'm not alone. In the year of hurricanes and weddings, I married my wife.

A queer wedding in Florida is an event not unlike a hurricane; it's something that can cause storm clouds to gather, boiling like lava on the horizon of a very red state. But we invited everyone we love. All of our friends—essentially, our shared family—an extension of our community. Texas, New York, Washington, California, Louisiana. Even folks from Norway showed up. Almost 90 percent of our guests came from out of state. We wanted to show them a version of our home that was different from what they'd come to expect about Orlando (theme parks and mouse ears). We wanted our friends to know that we live here too, and that means it's a place specifically for gay people. If I live and love here, how can it not be? My friends helped us decorate for the reception, brought out the champagne for us to toast, and made contributions to a fund for LGBTQ+ Florida youth at our request. Our wedding wasn't just celebrating the two of us. It was celebrating how queer people make Florida a better place.

Although my biological family lives in Florida, they were not invited to the wedding. It can be hard to explain to people why it's easier to form community with the family I've collected versus the one that I was born into. They want to know: *Doesn't it make you sad? Don't you wish things could be different?*

Sadness is subjective. In a world of wishes, nothing is real. The promise of love is worthless without any action to back it up. Cruel twist of fate: I learned that in church.

All of the things that I wanted from my biological family—to feel supported, respected, and truly seen for who I am as a person—happen with ease when it comes to the people I surround myself with. My chosen family is a group of individuals who continually give; they see who I am and celebrate me for exactly that reason. No one asks me to hide my queerness. It's encouraged. It's loved. I've known my best friend for over a decade and her brother for almost that long. His friends—people he'd met who became his family—have now become my family, too. We stay at each other's homes, we walk each other's dogs, we call each other first with good and bad news alike. There are dinner parties where everyone's in the kitchen cooking, Fourth of July barbecues, birthday pool parties, and Easters spent celebrating each other in lieu of the Lord. When my very first book was published, these friends threw a party and made my favorite kinds of food, brought me my favorite brand of beer, and showed up for every reading and book event I hosted in town. We all live within twenty-five minutes of each other, and when we have to move, the entire group arrives in grubby clothes to help load the truck. There's no need for grand gestures; it's a lot of small moments built on top of each other that allow me to feel fully loved. There is nothing I wouldn't do for these friends. They continue to do everything for me.

In the past year, I got married, but I also dealt with massive hurricanes that flooded the streets, took out our power, caused a tree to crack in half and nearly smash through the roof of our house. Hurricane seasons stretch longer each year, and for the first time in memory, we had to navigate a hurricane at the end of October. While people in other regions of the country were planning their Halloween costumes, Floridians were stocking up on nonperishables, filling our tubs with water, and organizing for mass power outages. This might seem harrowing, but for many of us down here, it's become the terrible norm. My loved ones did all this planning, together, and at the same time, I was preparing to officiate my friends' wedding—the friends who'd supported us through our own wedding earlier in the year by catering our event, planning music for the DJ, and coordinating our clothes in matching color schemes. Storm after storm, these were the friends who'd helped us with pet care, and shared their stash of wine and snacks when our hurricane supplies ran dry. They offered showers and bathrooms and cold water and phone chargers, and we've done the same when our household got power back and others did not. They'd asked me to stand up with them. To be part of their vows and their love.

Toasts were given, glasses raised. Memories recounted. All the times we'd held each other, made each other laugh and cry. A wedding is a celebration of a couple in love, but it's also a community offering up resources and reminding us that we don't move through the world alone. We took family photos with our friends after the ceremony. We brought each other drinks, shared plates of cake, and threw our shoes in a corner so we could dance barefoot. We swayed together with our arms around each other's shoulders, one big ball of love. Their wedding was our wedding. Their love was our love.

Part of growing up in Florida was learning what kind of weather I could withstand. For a long time, it was purely about survival. I navigated all kinds of storms with my biological family, battening down parts of myself that nearly wound up flattened in the process. But the reality of a hurricane is that it always comes to an end. Storms push through, smash things, destroy lives, and then miraculously depart. You're left with the aftermath, but there's also the sun. There's an opportunity to rebuild.

Each time I share a meal and a memory with my collected family, I discover a twinge of new greenery peeking up from my heart. The ways that we support each other in the moments directly following hardship show how every bad thing can be weathered, together.

I can't say I'll ever have a relationship with my biological family, but I'm not sure that matters. What I do value is the fact that I have a community of people who care if I'm happy and supported. Who accept me not only for who I am but also for who I aspire to become. They see the promise inside of me. They trust and believe I can do more, be more. Help more.

As time passes, I learn more about myself and my place in the world. I'm a small but important part of the larger whole. So much of my feeling this way is thanks to the people who want me to eagerly experience every weird, funny, and blissful moment of this short life. Because of them, I wake up and understand that regardless of what's on the horizon—wedding or hurricane—I can move through life knowing that I won't have to do any of it alone. The world may offer up a thunder cloud, but I know how to thrive inside it. All that rain makes the swamp I love best flourish and grow.

ABOUT THE CONTRIBUTORS

MARY ANNE ADAMS is a community activist, social worker, and public health community researcher. She is the founder and executive director of ZAMI NOBLA (National Organization of Black Lesbians on Aging) based in Atlanta, Georgia.

ALEX ALBERTO (they/them) is a queer author, publisher, and filmmaker. Their memoir, *Entwined: Essays on Polyamory and Creating Home*, explores their decade-long journey toward a nonnuclear family. Find Alex at alexalberto.com and @thatalexalberto.

KRISTEN ARNETT is the queer Floridian author of the novels *Stop Me If You've Heard This One* and *With Teeth.* Her debut novel, *Mostly Dead Things,* was a *New York Times* bestseller.

ELIZABETH HART BERGSTROM is a queer, chronically ill writer whose work appears in the *Bennington Review, Indiana Review, Michigan Quarterly Review, Passages North*, the *New York Times*, and elsewhere.

FRAN BIEDERMAN served as the secretary for the National Council of Teachers of English for thirty years. She is one of eight children raised by a single mother who taught them to care for others and help where they could.

RODNEY M. BORDEAUX is a member of the Rosebud Sioux Tribe/Oyate and has served as tribal president and as a member of the tribal council. He is committed to the advancement and self-sufficiency of the Sicangu Lakota.

SUANNE CARLSON is a cofounder of the 501(c)(3) charitable organization Homes on Wheels Alliance. Having lived nomadically since 2009, she has discovered unexpected community, purpose, and friendship among fellow travelers on the open road.

RHAINA COHEN is the best-selling author of *The Other Significant Others: Reimagining Life with Friendship at the Center* and an award-winning editor and producer for the NPR podcast *Embedded.*

JONATHAN ESCOFFERY is the author of the linked story collection *If I Survive You*, which was longlisted for the 2022 National Book Award and named a finalist for the 2023 Booker Prize.

HANK GAMEL, a US Air Force veteran, became the executive director of Hope Meadows in 2014, after retiring from a thirty-year police career. He also serves as the chairman of the board of Community Plus Federal Credit Union.

SIMONE GORRINDO is the author of the memoir *The Wives*, a finalist for the 2024 Washington State Book Awards. Her writing has also appeared in the *New York Times*, *New York Magazine*, and many others. She lives in Tacoma, Washington, with her husband and children.

HANNAH GRIECO is the author of *First Kicking, Then Not*, published by Stanchion Books in 2025. She writes a literary column for *Washington City Paper* and teaches English at Marymount University. Find her at www.hgrieco.com.

TIFFANY HARRIS is a global Jewish leader passionate about geopolitics, interfaith connection, coalition building, and empowering young adults. She serves as chief program officer at Mem Global.

GABRIELLE KORN is the author of *Everybody (Else) Is Perfect: How I Survived Hypocrisy, Beauty, Clicks, and Likes*; *Yours for the Taking*; and

The Shutouts. Her next nove, *Long Island Girls*, comes out in 2026. She lives in Los Angeles with her wife.

AMANDA E. MACHADO is a queer Mexican and Ecuadorian American writer and facilitator whose work has appeared in *Guernica*, *Slate*, *The Atlantic*, *The Guardian*, and many others.

SARAH THANKAM MATHEWS was born in India and is based in New York. Her debut novel *All This Could Be Different* was shortlisted for multiple prizes, including the National Book Award.

DANI MCCLAIN is an award-winning journalist and author of *We Live for the We: The Political Power of Black Motherhood*. She lives in Cincinnati, Ohio.

ADAM MEYER is an operations manager at a climate-focused start-up, a Nordic ski coach, and a dinner party host. He loves data and bringing people together.

JAKE MONTANO (he/they), an educator, creative, and organizer living in San Francisco, is also Imelda Glucose (she/her) of the Rice Rockettes. Together, they are a force for the good and groovy.

KIM STANLEY ROBINSON is an American science fiction writer. His most recent books are *The Ministry for the Future* and *The High Sierra: A Love Story*. His work has been translated into twenty-nine languages.

ADAM VITCAVAGE is the founder of the literary website *Debutiful*. His interviews and criticism have also appeared in *Electric Literature*, *Paste Magazine*, and *The Millions*. He lives in Denver, Colorado, with his wife.

KATE MADDEN YEE is a freelance writer in Northern California, where she has lived in cohousing since 2000. She loves to write about women, health, and spirituality.

ABOUT THE EDITOR

Samantha Paige Rosen's writing on identity, the arts, and culture has appeared in the *Washington Post*, *Harper's Bazaar*, *ELLE*, *Slate*, *Them*, *Literary Hub*, and elsewhere. She earned her BA from Smith College and her MFA from Sarah Lawrence College. Sam lives outside Philadelphia, where she is a freelance writer and editor, a writing tutor and coach, and an amateur potter. *Living, Together* is her first book.

ACKNOWLEDGMENTS

I knew it was going to be tough to compile the right contributors for an anthology around communal living and ways of being. How would I find people? How could I convince them to write or talk about their homes, lifestyles, and communities? A lot of brainstorming and sleuthing went into putting together the collection of voices here, but I was also connected to many of this book's contributors through friends of friends (of friends of friends). I smile when I think about that: What we are willing to do for one another makes a difference.

I am forever grateful to and in awe of this book's essayists and Q&A participants: Liz, Adam, Jonathan, Dani, Alex, Hannah, Rhaina, Suanne, Kate, Rodney, Tiffany, Gabrielle, Hank, Fran, Amanda, Stan, Simone, Mary Anne, Jake (and Imelda), Adam, Sarah, and Kristen. I learned so much from and truly enjoyed the many hours, drafts, and conversations. This is *our* book, and I hope you feel that. I owe everything to Liz, who wrote an essay that allowed me to send my book proposal to agents (and that made me cry the first time I read it). To the contributors who took the time to write essays and sit for interviews so I could have material to send out to editors—Hannah, Alex, Gabrielle, Tiffany, and Mary Anne—and to Stan, for generously lending your essay at that stage, thank you all for your faith in this project.

To Maggie Cooper, my dream agent: There's not a second of the day that I don't feel lucky for getting to work with you. You are a ray of sunshine, a comforting hug, the brightest lightbulb, an unofficial editor and sometimes unofficial therapist, inspirational in myriad ways, but especially for your swift email responses. I feel so cared for in your hands, and I know how exceptional that is. Thank you for the collaboration; I hope we get to do this again.

To my editor, Haley Lynch, for understanding why this particular book had to be an anthology. Thanks for the insights, compassion, and laughs that extended our meetings far beyond the scheduled times. And thank you to everyone at Beacon Press—Carol Chu, Beth Collins, Sanj Kharbanda, Susan Lumenello, Bev Rivero, Brittany Wallace, and any assistants who I haven't met but who've been involved in the process, as well as Emily Dolbear and Elena Rey—for treating *Living, Together* with such care. At every stage, I could tell this book was appreciated; it has meant so much.

Lilly Dancyger, Emma Copley Eisenberg, Marisa Franco, Sophie Lucido Johnson, and Casper ter Kuile—you said the nicest things about *Living, Toegther*! I so appreciate your kindness and your time.

To my first creative nonfiction professor, Kristen Cosby, for providing encouragement and hope during one of the hardest years of my life. I will never forget staying up into the wee hours of the morning writing for your class because I was more excited to write than anything else, or you telling me to "be ballsy" on the last day. (I've tried.) To my graduate school professors at Sarah Lawrence—Vinson Cunningham, Melissa Febos, Tim Kreider, Leigh Newman, Stephen O'Connor, David Ryan, Vijay Seshadri, and Alice Truax—as well as former program director Brian Morton and current director Paige Ackerson-Kiely. What a gift to have time with you then and to have your continued support now. Post-MFA, I've taken incredible classes through Grub Street with Sarah Jane Cody, and Blue Stoop with Jiordan Castle and Kristen Martin (x2)! Thank you to these organizations and individuals for providing accessible environments for continuous learning and community building. Thank you, also, to the peers I've been in workshop with over the past decade.

When I embarked on this anthology, I was new to the world of book publishing and I leaned on other writers and editors for guidance. Thank you to those who were kind enough to speak with me about book proposals, querying agents, possible contributors, publicity, and more. This includes fellow anthology editors Dahlia

Adler, Zoë Bossiere, Michele Filgate, Natalie Eve Garrett, Hannah Grieco, Loren Kleinman, Ilana Masad, Kelly McMasters, and Eliza Smith, as well as writers Alex Alberto, Gina Chung, Mac Crane, Alisha Gorder, Ruth Madievsky, Lena Moses-Schmitt, and Laura Sims. Resources from Eric Smith, Jane Friedman, and Emma Copley Eisenberg were invaluable. Thank you to Tajja Isen for publishing my essay on multigenerational living in *Catapult*, which was the spark for *Living, Together*, and for confirming early on that this book was a good idea.

At times it felt awkward reaching out to people, some of whom were strangers, asking whether they knew anyone who lives communally in specific locations or iterations, but so many people offered ideas. In particular, Alex Alberto, Kyle Casey Chu, Claire Denny, Rachel Garbus, Tim Kreider, Mia Marion, Courtney E. Martin, Stephanie Mathews, Maryka Paquette, Jennifer Rosen, Nina Sharma, and Adrian Shirk delivered. Thank you, truly.

It's probably not surprising that I'm a big collaborator, and this includes being eager for brainstorming opportunities and feedback. Samantha Allen, Hannah Grieco, Elizabeth Held, Kristen Martin, Rae Pagliarulo, Amelia Possanza, Theresa Sullivan, and basically my whole family (Jennifer Rosen, Elizabeth Cleckley, Patty Rosen, and Stuart Rosen)—I hope you know how important you were to this process. Thank you, also, to everyone who has been involved in publicity conversations and efforts.

This book wouldn't be real without Francesca Tomaino and Jiordan Castle. Francesca, you saw communal living as part of my life years before I did. Who knows where I'd be without you (and not just in the literary sense)? Jiordan, my cheerleader: Thanks for saying, "Are you *sure* you don't want to write a book?" Your belief in me literally made all the difference.

A lot of people listened to me talk about this anthology over the past several years. I so appreciate those who continued to ask, with genuine enthusiasm, "What's happening with the book?!": my pottery and a cappella friends, my students, and the Super Marcomm crew. Also, my loved ones outside these groups who've supported me from near and far for years. Thank you to Laura Piccoli for taking my author photos—we've been training for this moment since we were fifteen!—and to Nicole Geldart for the edits.

While working on *Living, Together*, I faced two unexpected and devastating losses. Deacon, my heart and soul in cat form, died months before I turned in my first draft. His always energetic sister Maisy died around the time I turned in my final draft. By dedicating the book to them, I want to acknowledge a form of family and home that is often discounted yet is irreplaceable. Their feline sibling Piper—who has been so attentive since my MFA days that she was awarded an honorary MFA (I don't make the rules!)—is still keeping me company, and I'm endlessly grateful to her. It was the privilege of my life to write surrounded by this trio of loving personalities for ten years, and I deeply miss those who are gone. Thanks to Fergal, my newest cat, for bringing my smile back. (I forgive you for the chaos you cause nightly.)

To my aunt, Jane Marion, for blazing the writing trail. To my grandma, Millie Meiman, for being so interested in everything I've done, but especially this. To my sister Elizabeth Cleckley for continuing to insist that the TV pilot I wrote when I was twenty-four is one of the best stories she's read, and for being the first person to read *Living, Together* in its entirety. To my sister Jennifer Rosen for engaging in so much book talk that we had to start referring to it as "b**k!" I love you all.

To my parents, Stuart and Patty Rosen, for absolutely everything.

To the readers of *Living, Together*: I hope you find what you're looking for in this b**k—and in each other.

CREDITS

"Hello to All This" by Gabrielle Korn was partially adapted from Gabrielle Korn, "I Wanted to Live in NYC Forever," *Coveteur*, December 14, 2022, https://coveteur.com/gabrielle-korn-leaving-nyc.

"Enough Is as Good as a Feast" by Kim Stanley Robinson was previously published by the University of Plymouth, August 25, 2018, https://blogs.plymouth.ac.uk/imaginingalternatives/2018/08/15/enough-is-as-good-as-a-feast-by-kim-stanley-robinson/.

NOTES

INTRODUCTION

1. Kathy Evans, "How Much the Middle Class Paid for Rent in the '90s Compared to Now," *GOBankingRates*, June 6, 2024, https://www.nasdaq.com/articles/how-much-middle-class-paid-rent-90s-compared-now.

2. Carolina Aragão et al., *The Modern American Family: Key Trends in Marriage and Family Life*, Pew Research Center, September 14, 2023, https://www.pewresearch.org/social-trends/2023/09/14/the-modern-american-family/.

3. Margot Kahn, "How and Why to Edit an Anthology: Addressing the Naysayers," JaneFriedman.com, November 27, 2017, https://janefriedman.com/how-to-edit-anthology/.

SURVIVAL OF THE CONNECTED

1. *Encyclopedia Britannica*, "Mutualism," https://www.britannica.com/science/mutualism-biology, accessed January 18, 2025.

2. Xerces Society, "About Bumble Bees," https://xerces.org/bumble-bees/about, accessed January 18, 2025.

3. US Forest Service, "Bumblebees," https://www.fs.usda.gov/wildflowers/pollinators/pollinator-of-the-month/bumblebees.shtml, accessed January 18, 2025.

4. *Encyclopedia Britannica*, "Commensalism," https://www.britannica.com/science/commensalism, accessed January 18, 2025.

5. David Rust, "Mycorrhizae Explained," North American Mycological Association, https://namyco.org/interests/education/mushroom-basics/, accessed June 24, 2025.

6. Diane Toomey, "Exploring How and Why Trees 'Talk' to Each Other," *Yale Environment 360*, September 1, 2016, https://e360.yale.edu/features/exploring_how_and_why_trees_talk_to_each_other.often.

7. Richard Grant, "Do Trees Talk to Each Other?" *Smithsonian*, March 2018, https://www.smithsonianmag.com/science-nature/the-whispering-trees-180968084/.

8. Sara Chodosh, "Ravens Are So Smart It's Actually Kind of Disconcerting, New Study Finds," *Popular Science*, July 15, 2017, https://www.popsci.com/ravens-smart-plan-ahead/; Ellen Blackstone (writer) and Michael Stein (narrator), "Raven's Love Song," *BirdNote*, February 14, 2022, https://www.birdnote.org/podcasts/birdnote-daily/ravens-love-song.

9. "Naturalist Notes: Wolves and Ravens," *Yellowstone Quarterly* (2020), https://www.yellowstone.org/naturalist-notes-wolves-and-ravens/.

10. Avery Hurt, "Why There's the Leader of the Wolf Pack," *Discover*, May 17, 2023, https://www.discovermagazine.com/planet-earth/why-theres-the-leader-of-the-wolf-pack.

11. Eva M. Krockow, "Is It Dangerous to Believe in a Just World?" *Psychology Today*, October 6, 2022, https://www.psychologytoday.com/us/blog/stretching-theory/202210/is-it-dangerous-believe-in-just-world.

12. D. W. Macdonald, "'Helpers' in Fox Society," *Nature* 282 (1979): 69–71, https://doi.org/10.1038/282069a0; Kelsey Kuhnhausen, "Orphaned Gosling Taken Under the Wing of a Recovering Canada Goose," Bird Alliance of Oregon, April 6, 2018, https://audubonportland.org/blog/orphaned-gosling-taken-under-the-wing-of-a-recovering-canada-goose/; Ellen Kalmbach, "Why Do Goose Parents Adopt Unrelated Goslings? A Review of Hypotheses and Empirical Evidence, and New Research Questions," *Ibis* 148 (January 2006): 66–78, https://doi.org/10.1111/j.1474-919X.2006.00496.x.

13. Hiroshi Ueno et al., "Helping-Like Behaviour in Mice Towards Conspecifics Constrained Inside Tubes," *Scientific Reports* 9 (2019): 5817, https://doi.org/10.1038/s41598-019-42290-y.

RENOVATIONS AND REBIRTHS

1. Jaeah Lee, "The Agony of Putting Your Life on Hold to Care for Your Parents," *New York Times*, March 28, 2023, https://www.nytimes.com/2023/03/28/magazine/elder-child-care-millennials.html.

Q&A WITH SUANNE CARLSON

1. Homes on Wheels Alliance, "RTR," https://homesonwheelsalliance.org/category/rtr/, accessed January 19, 2025.

2. Homes on Wheels Alliance, "WRTR," https://homesonwheelsalliance.org/category/wrtr/, accessed January 19, 2025.

3. Homes on Wheels Alliance, "HOWA eFund and Tent Programs" https://homesonwheelsalliance.org/nomad-emergency/, accessed May 26, 2025.

RETURNING TO OSPAYE

1. Philimon Two Eagle, oral traditions, Rosebud Sioux Sicangu Treaty Council, Rosebud, SD, 2005.

2. Donovan Arleigh Sprague, *Rosebud Sioux: Images of America* (Rapid City, SD: Arcadia, 2005), 8.

3. Victor Douville, "Makoce Kin III (The Land)," Sinte Gleska University, November 14, 2024.

HELLO TO ALL THIS

1. Joan Didion, *Slouching Towards Bethlehem* (New York: Noonday Press, 1990), 238.

Q&A WITH HANK GAMEL AND FRAN BIEDERMAN

1. Hope Meadows, https://hopemeadows.org/, accessed January 19, 2025.

2. Paige Sutherland, "Cut Off and Shut Out: The Reality of Illinois Foster Youths at 21," *MEDILL Reports Chicago*, Northwestern University, October 20, 2014 (page now discontinued).

THE MYTH OF STABLE GROUND

1. Kelly O'Mara, "Large Parts of the Bay Area Are Built on Fill. Why and Where?" KQED, February 6, 2020, https://www.kqed.org/news/11799297/large-parts-of-the-bay-area-are-built-on-fill-why-and-where.

2. Amber D. Haley et al., *Neighborhood-Level Determinants of Life Expectancy in Oakland, CA*, Center on Human Needs, Virginia Commonwealth University, 2012, https://societyhealth.vcu.edu/media/society-health/pdf/PMReport_Alameda.pdf; Elizabeth Fernandez, "Study Spotlights Bleak Eff ects of Poverty," *SFGate*, April 18, 2008, https://www.sfgate.com/bayarea/article/Study-spotlights-bleak-eff ects-of-poverty-3286906.php.

3. James Baldwin, *Giovanni's Room: A Novel* (New York: Dial Press, 1956), 92.

4. Sogorea Te' Land Trust, "Shuumi Land Tax," https://sogoreate-landtrust.org/shuumi-land-tax/, accessed January 19, 2025.

5. Jehan L. Roberson, "Tracing Harriet Tubman's Steps," *Medium*, October 28, 2018, https://medium.com/zora/tracing-harriet-tubmans-steps-e1a56f6fa073.

6. "State Regulators Unanimously Approve PG&E's 4th Rate Hike for 2024," ABC News, September 12, 2024, https://abc7news.com/post/pge-rate-hike-california-public-utilities-commission-unanimously-approves-6-monthly-increase-electricity-bills/15296646/.

7. Sarah Sax, "Black Families Passed Their Homes from One Generation to the Next. Now They May Be Lost," *The Guardian*, October 6, 2021, https://amp.theguardian.com/us-news/2021/oct/06/leading-cause-black-land-loss-how-climate-crisis-supercharging-dispossession.

8. Aurora Levins Morales, *Medicine Stories: Essays for Radicals* (Durham, NC: Duke University Press, 2019), 186.

9. Aubrey Streit Krug, "Grounded," in *What Kind of Ancestor Do You Want to Be?*, ed. John Hausdoerff er et al. (Chicago: University of Chicago Press, 2021), 22.

ENOUGH IS AS GOOD AS A FEAST

1. Warren Williams, *Energy and Community Planning: A Tale of Two Cities*, City of Davis, California, https://www.aceee.org/files/proceedings/1980-82/data/papers/1980_020.pdf, accessed June 24, 2025.

2. John Bartlett, *Familiar Quotations: A Collection of Passages, Phrases, and Proverbs Traced to Their Sources in Ancient and Modern Literature* (Boston: Little, Brown, 1905), 20.

Q&A WITH MARY ANNE ADAMS

1. Kristie L. Seelman, Mary Anne Adams, and Tonia Poteat, "Interventions for Healthy Aging Among Mature Black Lesbians: Recommendations Gathered Through Community-Based Research," *Journal of Women & Aging* 6, no. 29 (December 27, 2016): 530–42, https://doi.org/10.1080/08952841.2016.1256733.

DRAG IN THIS HOUSE

1. Trans Legislation Tracker, https://translegislation.com/, accessed January 31, 2025.
2. Abigail Fagan, "New Study Finds Half of LGBTQ+ Are Estranged from Family," *Psychology Today*, October 10, 2023, https://www.psychologytoday.com/us/blog/brothers-sisters-strangers/202310/new-study-finds-half-of-lgbtq-are-estranged-from-family.
3. Thaddeus Morgan, "How 19th-Century Drag Balls Evolved into House Balls, Birthplace of Voguing," History.com, June 28, 2021, https://www.history.com/articles/drag-balls-house-ballroom-voguing.
4. Nina Jackson Levin et al., "'We Just Take Care of Each Other': Navigating 'Chosen Family' in the Context of Health, Illness, and the Mutual Provision of Care Amongst Queer and Transgender Young Adults," *International Journal of Environmental Research and Public Health* 17, no. 19 (2020): 7346, https://doi.org/10.3390/ijerph17197346.
5. Tangela Roberts et al., "Building a Family: An Exploration of Queer Resilience Through the Formation of Family," in *Identity as Resilience in Minoritized Communities*, ed. Julie M. Koch et al. (Cham: Springer Nature Switzerland, 2023), https://doi.org/10.1007/978-3-031-38977-1_3.

THE OPPOSITE OF LONELINESS

1. Sarah Thankam Mathews, "Bed-Stuy Strong: How to Start a 3,000-Member Neighborhood Mutual Aid Network," *Autostraddle*, June 4, 2020, https://www.autostraddle.com/bed-stuy-strong-how-to-start-a-3000-member-neighborhood-mutual-aid-network/.
2. Kristin Ross, *The Commune Form: The Transformation of Everyday Life* (New York: Verso Books, 2024).